AS
TIME RUNS
OUT

A SIMPLE GUIDE TO BIBLE PROPHECY

AS TIME RUNS OUT

ROBERT JEFFRESS

BROADMAN
& HOLMAN
PUBLISHERS
Nashville, Tennessee

0-8054-2019-3

Published by Broadman & Holman Publishers, Nashville, Tennessee
Editorial Team: Vicki Crumpton, Janis Whipple, Kim Overcash
Page Design & Typesetting: PerfecType, Nashville, Tennessee

Dewey Decimal Classification: 220
Subject Heading: BIBLE—PROPHECIES / BIBLE—TEACHING
Library of Congress Card Catalog Number: 99-11117

Unless otherwise stated all Scripture citation is from the NASB, the New American Standard Bible, © the Lockman Foundation, 1960, 1962, 1963, 1968, 1971, 1972, 1973, 1975, 1977, used by permission.

Published in association with Yates & Yates, Literary Agency, Orange, CA.

Library of Congress Cataloging-in-Publication Data
Jeffress, Robert, 1955–
    As time runs out: a simple guide to Bible prophecy / Robert Jeffress.
       p. cm.
    Includes bibliographical references.
    ISBN 0-8054-2019-3 (pbk.)
    1. Bible—Prophecies—End of the world. 2. End of the World—Biblical teaching. I. Title.
    BS649.E63J44 1999
    220.1'5—dc21

                                             99-11117
                                             CIP

1 2 3 4 5 03 02 01 00 99

Dedication

To Mark and Patty Lovvorn

Whether on the set of *Let's Make a Deal* or at the graves of our loved ones, you have stood by us through the happiest and saddest times of our lives. Thank you for your faithful friendship through the years.

Table of Contents

Why Study Prophecy?

Have you ever read the novel *Futility* by Morgan Robertson? The book tells the story of a magnificent ocean liner named the *Titan* that strikes an iceberg on its maiden voyage from Southampton to New York and sinks in the middle of the ocean. You are probably thinking, *This sure does sound like the real story of the* Titanic. Yet Robertson's novel differs from the actual event in several ways. The ship in *Futility* was 1,800 feet long while the real *Titanic* was 1,882 feet long. The *Titan* was able to displace 66,000 tons of water, while the Titanic was able to displace 70,000 tons of water. Yet, both ships were triple-screw ocean liners that could travel up to 25 knots per hour and transport 3,000 passengers.

You might wonder why Morgan Robertson would bother to write a novel that so closely approximated a real-life event. And why go to the trouble of varying some of the facts ever so slightly, including the name of the ship? The reason is quite simple. The *Titanic* sank on April 14, 1912. The novel *Futility* was published in 1898—fourteen years before the actual event![1]

It is amazing to think that a book written more than a decade earlier could so accurately forecast a historical event like the *Titanic*. But it is even more fascinating to realize that the Bible is able to foretell with laserlike accuracy events that will occur hundreds and even thousands of years after it was written. One can hardly turn a page of Scripture without finding some reference to a future event. Yet despite the vast amount of literature devoted to prophetic themes, few Christians have a clear understanding of the events that will lead to the return of Jesus Christ. Maybe you are one of those Christians who:

- reaches for a Tylenol when your "Read through the Bible" plan lands you in the Book of Daniel;
- thinks about changing churches when your pastor announces a yearlong study in the book of Revelation;
- breaks out in a cold sweat if a new Christian asks you to explain briefly the terms *rapture, tribulation,* and *millennium;*
- wonders why you should purchase this book instead of *Seven Scintillating Secrets for a Sensual Marriage.*

Why People Resist Studying Biblical Prophecy

Evangelist Billy Graham once observed that "the most neglected teaching in the church today is the Second Coming of Jesus Christ."[2] Why is that? As I have talked with both pastors

2

and laypeople about prophecy, I have discovered four major reasons people don't study Bible prophecy.

1. "The subject is too confusing to understand."

Most Christians are convinced that you must possess a seminary degree (or at least some skill in reading tea leaves) to comprehend the events surrounding the return of Jesus Christ. Not long ago I was visiting with the pastor of one of the largest churches in the denomination in which I serve. This man has an earned Ph.D. from a respected seminary and preaches to thousands of people each week. He said, "Robert, would you please write a simple book explaining Bible prophecy so that people like me can understand it?" If this doctor of theology feels inadequate to understand prophecy, no wonder the thousands in his congregation will never hear a series of messages on books of the Bible like Daniel and Revelation.

One of my closest friends in our church is convinced that God never meant for us to understand prophecy. "If God really wanted us to understand these things, why didn't He make them clearer in Scripture?" My response is, "God *has* clearly explained end-time events in Scripture." As an example, I directed his attention to Matthew 24–25.

As Jesus and His disciples were leaving the Temple, Jesus remarked that one day every stone of that magnificent place of worship would be torn down. Shaken at such a statement, the disciples asked the obvious question:

> Tell us, when will these things be, and what will
> be the sign of Your coming, and of the end of the
> age? (Matt. 24:3)

We know from history that about forty years after the disciples' question, the Roman conqueror Titus entered Jerusalem and destroyed the Temple. But it is clear from their question that this is not the only event with which they were concerned. They also wanted to know when Christ would return and what signs would precede His return and the end of the age. Notice what Jesus did *not* say in reply to their inquiry:

> "Boys, there is no way you could understand these events—especially you, Peter!"

> or

> "This is nothing you need to concern yourselves with. Trust me, everything will 'pan out' in the end."

> or

> "You shouldn't care about the end-time events. All you should be concerned with is sharing the gospel with as many people as possible."

Instead, Jesus answered the disciples' question with a lengthy explanation concerning end-time events. Although Jesus refused to answer the question "when" (in verse 36, Jesus confessed that even *He* did not know when these events would occur), He clearly answered "what" will happen:

> And Jesus answered and said to them, "See to it that no one misleads you. For many will come in My name, saying, 'I am the Christ,' and will mislead many. And you will be hearing of wars and

rumors of wars; see that you are not frightened, for those things must take place, but that is not yet the end. . . . Therefore when you see the ABOMINA- TION OF DESOLATION which was spoken of through Daniel the prophet, standing in the holy place" (let the reader understand), "then let those who are in Judea flee to the mountains; . . . But imme- diately after the tribulation of those days THE SUN WILL BE DARKENED, AND THE MOON WILL NOT GIVE ITS LIGHT, AND THE STARS WILL FALL from the sky, and the powers of the heavens will be shaken, and then the sign of the Son of Man will appear in the sky, and then all the tribes of the earth will mourn, and they will see the SON OF MAN COMING ON THE CLOUDS OF THE SKY with power and great glory." (Matt. 24:4–6, 15–16, 29–30)

At the end of chapter 3, we will discover that Matthew 24–25 gives us a simple outline of the end-time events that include the Great Tribulation, the return of Christ, the judg- ments, and Christ's rule on the earth.

2. "No one can know when Christ will return."

Bill and Janet are friends of ours who keep up with the latest fads in *eschatology* (a word describing the study of end- time events). Several years ago they took seriously Edgar Whiesnant's prediction that the Rapture (an event explained in the next chapter) was slated for 1988. However, they decided to prepare for this event in a most unusual way: They drained their savings account, loaded their van, and headed for—not the Millennial Kingdom—but the Magic Kingdom in Orlando, Florida.

I will admit that their response to the return of Christ was unique; nevertheless, it illustrates one reason so many people are skeptical about a study of the end times. Bible prophecy "experts" have turned a lot of people off to the subject of studying the end times by violating a basic principle in Scripture: We never are to set dates concerning the Second Coming of Christ. No one knows the date *any* prophetic event will occur.

The Old Testament prophet Daniel did not know when the end would come:

> And he [an angel of the Lord] said, "Go your way, Daniel, for these words are concealed and sealed up until the end time." (Dan. 12:9)

Although the apostle Paul probably thought he would live to see the end-time events unfold, he confessed that the day of the Lord would come unexpectedly:

> Now as to the times and the epochs, brethren, you have no need of anything to be written to you. For you yourselves know full well that the day of the Lord will come just like a thief in the night. (1 Thess. 5:1–2)

Even Jesus Christ Himself admitted that He had no idea when He would return:

6

> But of that day and hour no one knows, not even
> the angels of heaven, nor the Son, but the Father
> alone. (Matt. 24:36)

Last week I was traveling to Los Angeles. I arrived at the airport late in the evening and needed a shuttle to take me to the hotel. I called the shuttle service and asked when the next van would be available. Although they could not tell me when the van would arrive, they told me what to watch for—a blue van marked "SkyLark" that had a sign reading "Wilshire." During the next twenty minutes many vans stopped in front of the loading zone—orange vans, white vans, red vans. There were even a number of blue SkyLark vans with signs reading "Disneyland" or "Hollywood." Had I boarded any of those vans I would not have arrived safely at my destination. However, eventually the right van with the right sign arrived, and I knew to get on. Why? Even though I had not been told *when,* I had been told *what* to look for.

In the same way, none of us knows when the Lord will return. Nevertheless, God has given us a clear indication of what to look for so that we will not be deceived by those false christs that have appeared in every generation.

3. "There are too many different interpretations for prophecy to be that important."

Many years ago I was on a panel answering questions about theology. On the panel with me was a well-known speaker and author on the subject of apologetics. When someone asked a question concerning prophecy, he said, "I had better let Robert answer this one. You see, I am not a premillennialist, postmillenialist, or an amillennialist. I am a *panmillennialist.* I believe everything will pan out in the end." Chuckle, chuckle.

Granted, there are a number of differing interpretations concerning the end-time events. If you have been confused by terms like *premillennialist, postmillennialist,* and *amillennialist* or *pretribulation* rapture and *posttribulation* rapture, this book will help you to understand these often confusing terms. Nevertheless, the fact that there are a number of different interpretations about end-time events does not mean there is not one correct interpretation.

Perhaps you just cringed when you read the phrase "one correct interpretation." That's understandable. We live in an age in which anyone who claims his or her interpretation to be the "correct" interpretation is viewed with suspicion and disdain. How many times have you heard people say that "everyone is free to interpret the Bible as he chooses"? That statement is true—but only partially true. While everyone has the freedom to draw his or her own conclusions about the Bible, not everyone's interpretation is equally valid—especially when it involves the subject of Bible prophecy. Consider the words of the apostle Peter:

> But know this first of all, that no prophecy of
> Scripture is a matter of *one's own interpretation,* for
> no prophecy was ever made by an act of human
> will, but men moved by the Holy Spirit spoke
> from God. (2 Pet. 1:20–21, Author emphasis)

Don't allow the variety of opinions concerning prophecy to cause you to throw up your hands in despair. (Can you think of any issue in the Bible about which *everyone* agrees?) Although many of the details about end-time events are concealed, and therefore open to speculation, the Bible gives us a clear outline of the events that will lead to the return of Christ.

4. "Bible prophecy has nothing to do with everyday life."

Admittedly, most people are not nearly as concerned with the beast described in Revelation 13 as they are with the beast for whom they work five days a week at the office. Trying to make it through one jam-packed week of work, soccer practices, homework, and church activities is difficult enough without trying to figure out the mystery of the seventy weeks described in Daniel 9. Why should I worry about some future tribulation when I have plenty of my own problems right now?

Yet knowing where we are going in the future should greatly impact how we live in the present. For example, the highway department in our state has decided to construct a major, double-deck expressway through the center of our city. Although they have not announced when they will begin the project, all of the restaurant owners and small businesses that line the present highway are beginning to sell their property and relocate. Why? The new thoroughfare will reroute traffic away from their establishments, ensuring their demise if they remain. Even though these small businesses do not know when these future events will transpire, the fact that it is going to happen demands immediate action.

The same principle applies to biblical prophecy. God has clearly revealed what awaits Earth and all of her inhabitants. A major reconstruction project is guaranteed. The certainty of the return of Christ, the destruction of the present Earth, and every person's individual judgment by God should motivate us to action *now*. Abraham Lincoln once said, "If we could first tell where we are and where we are heading, we could better tell what to do and how to do it."

Why You Should Study Bible Prophecy

Hopefully you have discovered some answers to the objections you have heard from others (or may have had yourself) to studying Bible prophecy. But you may still be wondering why you should invest both your money and your time in a book like this. Here are a few reasons the investment will be worth it.

1. Bible Prophecy Is a Major Theme in the Bible

In Bible study there is a principle referred to as "The Law of Proportion." This law simply says that you can tell the importance of a certain subject in Scripture by how much space is devoted to it. Applying this principle to prophecy, we discover that more than one-fourth of the Bible consists of prophecy. In the Old Testament there are over 1,800 references to the return of Christ. Of the 260 chapters in the New Testament, there are more than 300 references to the Lord's return—one out of every 30 verses. Twenty-three of the 27 New Testament books give prominence to this subject. For every prophecy in Scripture concerning Christ's first coming, there are eight on Christ's second coming.

Both the proportion and prominence of the prophetic theme in Scripture argue for its importance.

2. An Understanding of Prophecy Helps Us Interpret and Apply the Bible Accurately

A knowledge of end-time events gives us a framework on which to hang the rest of Scripture. I believe that it is impossible to interpret and apply the Bible properly without a basic understanding of prophecy. Let me illustrate what I mean by examining a passage from the Old Testament prophet Isaiah:

> No longer will there be in it an infant who lives
>   but a few days,
> Or an old man who does not live out his days;
> For the youth will die at the age of one hundred
> And the one who does not reach the age of one
>   hundred
> Shall be thought accursed. (Isa. 65:20)

What period of time is in view here when there will be no infant mortality and people will live to be one hundred years of age? Obviously, this was not true in Isaiah's lifetime or in ours. Today infants die daily, and only a few adults live to have their birthdays announced by Willard Scott.

Some might believe that Isaiah is describing life in heaven. Yet Isaiah says that people will die after the age of one hundred. Will there be death in heaven? Revelation 21:4 promises that in heaven "there shall no longer be any death."

So if Isaiah is not referring to our life now or our life in heaven, what period of time is in view here? Isaiah was looking forward to Christ's rule on earth during a period we call the Millennium, which is described in numerous Old Testament and New Testament prophecies. As we will see in future chapters, this will be a unique time in world history when Christ will reign from David's throne in Jerusalem for one thousand years. Although it is difficult to comprehend, some believers during this period will possess their resurrection bodies; but other believers (the Tribulation saints) will enter the Millennium in their natural bodies and be subject to death (see chapter 8 for further discussion). It is this period of time that Isaiah is describing. Yet, without a basic understanding of the Millennium, it is impossible to comprehend this prophecy.

A basic understanding of Bible prophecy not only helps us to interpret the Bible correctly, but also to apply it accurately. Consider these familiar words of Jesus Christ:

> "For I was hungry, and you gave Me something to eat; I was thirsty, and you gave Me drink; I was a stranger, and you invited Me in; naked, and you clothed Me; I was sick, and you visited Me; I was in prison, and you came to Me." Then the righteous will answer Him, saying, "Lord, when did we see You hungry, and feed You, or thirsty, and give You drink?" . . . And the King will answer and say to them, "Truly I say to you, to the extent that you did it to one of these brothers of Mine, even the least of them, you did it to Me." (Matt. 25:35–37, 40)

How many times have you heard someone quote this passage and then make the application that the purpose of the church is to feed the hungry, clothe the naked, and visit the lonely? Several weeks ago I took our choir and orchestra with me to conduct a service at a prison facility. It was one of the most moving worship experiences in which I have ever participated. We saw dozens of prisoners place their trust in Christ and many others recommit their lives to the Lord. After the emotionally charged service, one of the choir members said to me, "Pastor, now I know what Jesus meant in Matthew 25 when he talked about visiting the prisoners."

While we should treat less fortunate people with Christlike compassion, Jesus was not addressing me or any Christian living at this present time in Matthew 25. If you look at the context of these verses, you will discover they are part of the Olivet Discourse that begins in Matthew 24 and describes the events that will lead to the return of Christ. In Matthew 25:31–45, Jesus explained the standard by which He will judge those who survive the Tribulation when He returns. They will be judged by how they treated the 144,000 Jewish witnesses during the Tribulation. For a person living in the Tribulation to clothe, feed, or comfort one of these witnesses would be a sign of his salvation, since it would be tantamount to ministering to Christ Himself.

Even though these verses refer to a specific group of people living in a future period of time, Christians freely take these verses out of context and attempt to apply them to the church today. While ministering to those who are hurting is both noble and Christlike, it is not the primary mission of the church. An understanding of prophecy is necessary to interpret and apply the Bible correctly.

3. An Understanding of Bible Prophecy Motivates Us toward Godly Living

The Bible never divorces prophetic truth from practical application. In 2 Peter 3, the apostle described the return of Christ, the destruction of the earth, and the creation of a new heaven and a new earth. But then he added these words:

> Since all these things are to be destroyed in this way, what sort of people ought you to be in holy conduct and godliness, looking for and hastening the coming of the day of God. (2 Pet. 3:11–12a)

I once heard Chuck Swindoll tell of an incident when former President Dwight Eisenhower was vacationing in Denver and his attention was drawn to an open letter in a local newspaper. Six-year-old Paul Hailey, dying of cancer, had expressed a wish to see the president of the United States.

Spontaneously, in one of those gracious gestures remembered long after a president's speeches are forgotten, the president decided to grant the boy's request. One Sunday morning in August, a big limousine pulled up outside the Hailey home and out stepped the president of the United States. Eisenhower walked up to the door and knocked. Donald Hailey, the father, opened the door. He was wearing blue jeans, an old shirt, and a day's growth of beard. Behind him was little Paul. Their amazement of finding President Eisenhower on their doorstep could hardly be imagined.

"Paul," said the president, "I understand you wanted to see me. I'm glad to see you, Paul."

The president shook Paul's hand, and the two walked together and conversed for a while. They shook hands again, and the president departed.

The Haileys and their neighbors talked about this kind and thoughtful deed of the president for years afterward. Only one person was not entirely happy about it—Mr. Hailey. He could never forget how he was dressed when he opened the door.

"Old jeans, that faded shirt, my unshaven face. What a way to greet the president of the United States," he lamented.

I can tell you something even more embarrassing than that. One day the sky will part, the trumpet will sound, and Jesus Christ will suddenly appear. Unfortunately, many Christians will not be properly "dressed" for His return. They will be wrapped up in the faded clothes of materialism, immorality, and personal ambition instead of the bright linen clothes of righteousness described in Revelation 19:8.

Let me ask you a personal question: If the Lord were to return today, would you be embarrassed by your appearance? If so, I pray that this study of the end times will be a powerful incentive for you to clothe yourself in "holy conduct" and "godliness" as we look forward to His certain return.

Promises, Promises

*I*magine that a friend says, "John Grisham's new novel is the best book I have ever read. You must get a copy and read it immediately." Taking your friend's advice, you purchase Grisham's latest lawyer tale and, after the kids are tucked in bed, sit down in your favorite chair and begin to read. You first turn to the middle of the book. Suddenly you are confronted with names, locations, and actions that make no sense whatsoever. Who in the world are "Bill" or "Joan" or "Judge Mills"? And what are they doing in the Caribbean? And why does Bill suddenly dump one million dollars over the edge of his boat? Confused, you decide to turn to the end of the book to discover the answers. "Joan" and "Judge Mills" are at Bill's funeral.

"You know, Joan, Bill should not have dumped that money over the side of his boat," the judge reflected.

"I know, Judge. But how did Bill know that the Mafia had been following him?" Joan inquired.

Now you are more confused than ever, so you put the book down in disgust. "Grisham has obviously lost his touch. Why can't he write a more coherent book?" you complain to your friend.

I realize that this absurd scenario is about as subtle as a sledgehammer, and yet it illustrates why so many people have difficulty understanding the subject of Bible prophecy: they start reading the book in the wrong place. If you want to make sense out of the Bible, the place to start is not in the last book of the Bible (Revelation), or in the middle of the book (Daniel or Ezekiel), but at the beginning of the book. In fact, the name of the first book of the Bible can be translated "beginnings." We call it Genesis, and it is the foundation for understanding Bible prophecy.

Tracing Our Spiritual Roots

Whenever we think of the Book of Genesis, we think of the landmark events that marked the beginning of civilization: Creation, the Fall, the first murder, the Flood, and the Tower of Babel. And yet, amazingly, these momentous events are compressed into just eleven chapters of Genesis. It is as if God were saying, "By the way, this is how the world got into the mess it is in now." And that is the theme of Genesis 1–11: man's alienation from God. In these opening chapters of Genesis, you see man moving farther and farther away from God until his act of rebellion at the Tower of Babel.

But beginning in Genesis 12, and extending through the Book of Revelation, we see God's reconciliation with man. Although God would have been completely justified in destroying the world after the fiasco at Babel, He announced a plan that would result in salvation, instead of condemnation, to those who were willing to believe. An important figure in God's rescue plan for humanity is a man named Abraham. And the remaining thirty-nine chapters of Genesis focus on this one man and his family. Why is so much attention given to Abraham and his family? Because understanding God's promise to Abraham is the key to understanding the rest of the Bible and the end times.

An Unlikely Hero

In the concluding verses of Genesis 11, we find Abraham and his family living in the city of Ur of the Chaldeans (Gen. 11:27–28). Ur was a major commercial city in Mesopotamia. It was comparable in stature to New York or London today. When I was in college, I remember traveling to the University of Texas to view an exhibition of some of the amazing artifacts discovered at Ur, revealing that its citizens were proficient in mathematics, astronomy, and engraving. But the archaeologist's spade has also unearthed the fact that the residents of Ur were idol worshipers.

While we would like to think that Abraham was different from the pagans with whom he lived, Scripture tells us he was not. Joshua 24:2–3 clearly showed that Abraham was also an idolater when the Lord appeared to him:

And Joshua said to all the people, "Thus says the LORD, the God of Israel, 'From ancient times your

fathers lived beyond the River, namely, Terah, the
father of Abraham and the father of Nahor, and
they served other gods. Then I took your father
Abraham from beyond the River, and led him
through all the land of Canaan, and multiplied his
descendants and gave him Isaac.'" (Author
emphasis)

Allow me to stop for a moment and remind you of the
wonderful truth concerning God's grace. If you are a Christian,
your coming to Christ had absolutely *nothing* to do with your
goodness, but it had everything to do with *God's* goodness. Titus
3:5 tells us that "[God] saved us, not on the basis of deeds
which we have done in righteousness, but according to His
mercy." God's choice of Abraham was not based on his righteousness—he was just as wicked as any resident of Ur—but on
God's undeserved mercy.

Thus, God appeared to this idol worshiper and issued
this command:

Go forth from your country,
And from your relatives
And from your father's house,
To the land which I will show you. (Gen. 12:1)

God was telling Abraham to leave everything familiar to
him—his country, his friends, his family—to travel to an
unknown destination. Just this past week we had dinner with a
new family in our church who could have identified with
Abraham. Two years ago they were living in their native country of Mexico. Both the husband and wife had fabulous jobs,

they had just completed a beautiful home, and they had recently learned they were going to have a child. *Life doesn't get much better than this,* they thought!

Yet, God had a different plan in mind. A series of sudden difficulties at work convinced this couple that God was leading them to come to the United States, even though neither one of them spoke a word of English. But they knew God had spoken. So they quit their jobs, abandoned their spacious new home, and traveled to this country with nothing more than what they could carry in their suitcases. That takes faith!

It is that same kind of faith God was asking Abraham to exercise. And yet, with the command came a wonderful promise. As the great biographer F. B. Meyer said, God's commands are not always accompanied by reason, but they are accompanied by promises, either spoken or unspoken. In Abraham's case, God followed his command to Abraham with a clear promise:

> Go . . .
> To the land which I will show you;
> And I will make you a great nation,
> And I will bless you,
> And make your name great;
> And so you shall be a blessing;
> And I will bless those who bless you,
> And the one who curses you I will curse.
> And in you all the families of the earth shall be
>   blessed. (Gen. 12:1–3)

Promises of the Covenant

Let's take a moment to examine closely the three ele-ments of this promise to Abraham, which theologians call the Abrahamic Covenant.

1. *A land.* "Go forth from your country . . . To the land which I will show you" (12:1). God promised to Abraham and his descendants a land that would belong to them forever. Later, in Genesis 15:18–21, God gave the specific boundaries of the land that would belong to Israel. Although Israel does not yet inhabit all of this land, the Bible promises that one day they will. The basis for the conflict in the Middle East today is Israel's conviction that this land belongs to them because of God's promise to Abraham.

2. *A seed.* "And I will make you a great nation, And I will bless you" (12:2). God also promised Abraham that he would be the father of a great nation whose descendants would be as innumerable as the stars in the sky or the sand on the seashore (Gen. 22:17). This is a particularly amazing prophecy consider-ing the fact that Abraham was seventy-five years old (Heb. 11:12 describes him as being "as good as dead") and was mar-ried to a barren wife (cp. Gen. 11:30).

3. *A blessing.* "And in you all the families of the earth shall be blessed" (12:3b). This promise is the obvious climax of God's covenant with Abraham. What did God mean that the entire world would be blessed through Abraham? Some say the fact that Christians, Muslims, and Jews claim Abraham as their spir-itual father is a fulfillment of this prophecy. Abraham certainly has been a spiritual blessing to much of the religious world.

But the blessing God had in mind here is much more specific. God was promising that one of Abraham's descendants

21

would be the Savior of the world who would forever remove the curse of sin and death. This promise was a clear prediction of the coming of Christ.

I will admit that in the past, I had difficulty seeing Jesus Christ in this promise. The theological tradition in which I was trained claimed that Abraham would not and could not have had a clear understanding of the coming of Messiah. Abraham trusted God for a land, a seed, and some general blessing, not for a specific Savior. So what changed my mind? Reading the Bible! In Galatians 3, Paul claimed that Abraham clearly understood that the blessing mentioned in Genesis 12:3 was directly tied to the coming of Christ.

Before we look at Galatians 3, a little background information might be helpful. Paul wrote this letter to refute the teaching of a group known as the Judaizers, who had infected the churches of Galatia. The Judaizers, like so many religious groups today, were teaching that faith in Christ is necessary, but not sufficient, to save a person. "A person must trust in Christ *and* keep the law to be saved." Paul was reminding the Galatians that it is faith in Christ *alone* that saves us. To demonstrate that truth Paul pointed to Abraham. Abraham? Didn't he live thousands of years before Christ? Yes, but he was still saved by trusting in a God who would exchange Abraham's sin for His righteousness.

> Even so Abraham BELIEVED GOD, AND IT WAS RECK-
> ONED TO HIM AS RIGHTEOUSNESS. Therefore, be sure
> that it is those who are of faith who are sons of
> Abraham. And the Scripture, foreseeing that God
> would justify the Gentiles by faith, *preached the
> gospel beforehand to Abraham,* saying, "ALL THE

NATIONS SHALL BE BLESSED IN YOU." (Gal. 3:6–8,
Author emphasis)

Do you see it? God promised Abraham that a Savior was
coming. And it was Abraham's faith in that promise that caused
God to reckon righteousness to Abraham. Here in Texas we use
the term *reckon* in a difference sense ("I reckon it's time to go").
But the Greek word translated "reckon" is an accounting term
that means "to put to one's account." If you give me a check for
$100 and I deposit it into my bank account, the teller performs
an accounting transaction whereby your $100 becomes *my*
$100. When Abraham believed in the promise of a Savior, God
exchanged Abraham's faith for righteousness and deposited that
righteousness into Abraham's spiritual bank account. From that
point on, God viewed Abraham as "not guilty" because of his
faith in God's provision for his sin.

Perhaps this illustration will help you understand this concept of reckoning. Suppose you want to purchase a home, and,
like most of us, you need a loan from the bank. Before the loan
officer will give you the loan, he asks to see your financial statement revealing how much money you have in the bank, a list of
your other assets, and a list of your debts. Unfortunately, your
financial statement looks horrible: you recently lost your job, you
are swimming in debt, and you have only two dollars in your
account! No banker in his right mind would loan you money
based on your financial statement ("I reckon you're out of luck!").

That's the bad news. But the good news is that Bill Gates
is your father, and his financial statement is in great shape! Out
of generosity Dad says to you, "If you would like, I will assume
responsibility for your debt. The bank can look to me for the

payment. Instead of submitting your financial statement, you can submit mine."

How would you respond to such an offer? If you were filled with pride and stupidity, you might say, "Forget it, Dad. I don't need your help. I can do it on my own. I'll just take my chances with the bank and see if I can't qualify for the loan." And guess what would happen? The bank would look at your financial statement and say, "No deal."

However, you could say, "Dad, I need your help. I've made some bad decisions, I'm practically bankrupt, but I really need that home. I will accept your gracious offer and allow you to take responsibility for this loan." And so, instead of submitting your pitiful financial statement for consideration, you present your dad's. Your application for a new home is not based on your resources but on his. And Dad's billions are more than sufficient to secure the needed loan.

Now that simple melodrama illustrates the most profound truth in the universe: God's universal laws demand that if you are going to secure a home in heaven you must be absolutely perfect. Your righteousness must be equal to that of Jesus Christ. You must obey God's laws perfectly. The problem is that all of us are morally and spiritually bankrupt. We don't have enough righteousness in our spiritual bank account to qualify for heaven. You may have more righteousness in your account than I do; I may have more in my account than Adolf Hitler had in his; but none of us has enough. As the Bible says, "For all have sinned and fall short of the glory of God" (Rom. 3:23).

Fortunately, we have a generous Father who has made us a great offer. "If you would like," God says, "I will consider your application for heaven, not based on your righteousness, but according to the righteousness of My son Jesus Christ." And when we trust in Christ's sacrificial death for our sins, God credits or "reckons" our spiritual bank account with the righteousness of Jesus Christ.

Galatians 3 explains that Abraham was saved the same way any of us are saved: by faith in the sacrificial death of Jesus Christ. Abraham looked forward to it; we look back at it. But it is faith in God's provision for our sin that causes God to credit righteousness to our account.

Characteristics of the Covenant

We have seen that God's promise to Abraham included the promise of a land, a nation, and a spiritual blessing. One key to making sense out of Bible prophecy is to understand three characteristics of God's covenant with Abraham.

1. *Literal.* As we saw in the previous section, there was certainly a spiritual component in God's promise to Abraham, but that spiritual blessing does not negate the material nature of the covenant. When God promised to give Abraham and his descendants a land that would be their own, Abraham understood that promise to be a literal promise that involved *real* estate! How do I know? Again, by reading the Bible. Notice how Abraham responded after God's original promise of a land:

> So Abram went forth as the LORD had spoken to him; and Lot went with him. Now Abram was seventy-five years old when he departed from Haran. And Abram took Sarai his wife and Lot his

25

nephew, and all their possessions which they had accumulated . . . thus they came to the land of Canaan. (Gen. 12:4–5)

Abraham's immediate reaction to God's promise was to pack up and head out to that new land! Remember, there was no Mayflower or Bekins back then. Can you imagine how much "stuff" Abraham must have accumulated in his seventy-five years of life? (We have only been in our present home for six years, and our two-car garage doesn't have room for *one* car [or even a bicycle]. I can't fathom what it will look like after seventy-five years.) Why would Abraham make such an effort to move if the "land" God promised was a reference to some heavenly city in the afterlife?

Make no mistake about it. Abraham *was* looking forward to a heavenly home. The writer of Hebrews records that Abraham was "looking for the city which has foundations, whose architect and builder is God" (Heb. 11:10). But Abraham's heavenly focus did not conflict with his earthly pursuit. Abraham took God's promise at face value and acted accordingly by moving to that promised land.

2. *Eternal.* God's promise to Abraham and his descendants of a land, a nation, and a blessing was not limited by time. On several occasions when Abraham was plagued by doubt or discouragement, God repeated His original promise to Abraham. One of those times was in Genesis 13 after a conflict that had separated Abraham from his nephew Lot:

And the LORD said to Abram, after Lot had separated from him, "Now lift up your eyes and look from the place where you are, northward and southward and eastward and westward; for all the land which you see, I will give it to you and to your descendants *forever.*" (Gen. 13:14–15, Author emphasis)

We mere mortals have a difficult time with the concept of "forever." How long is eternity? Henry Willen Van Loon wrote, "High up in the north, in the land called Svithjod, there stands a rock. It is 100 miles high and 100 miles wide. Once every 1,000 years a little bird comes to this rock to sharpen its beak. When the rock has thus been worn away, then a single day of eternity will have gone by."[1] Obviously, God's promise to Abraham and his descendants would endure for a long time!

3. *Unconditional.* This is the most important characteristic of God's promise to Abraham for our understanding of prophecy. Many Christians will concede that God's promise to Abraham was a literal promise in its original form. However, because of Israel's subsequent disobedience and disbelief, some believe that God revoked His promise to Abraham and made the church the beneficiary of the covenant. Furthermore, they believe that these promises originally made to Israel have been transformed into spiritual blessings for the church: the "land" promised to Israel is now heaven for the church; the throne from which Messiah will rule is no longer located in Jerusalem but in heaven (or in our hearts); the promised reign of Christ upon the earth is being fulfilled right now as Christ rules in the lives of Christians instead of in a future Millennium (a one-thousand-year period of time we will discuss in the next chapter).

Now, I will admit that such reasoning *sounds* logical . . . and even biblical. God made numerous conditional promises to the Israelites. For example, consider Moses' words to the Israelites before they entered into the Promised Land:

> See, I am setting before you today a blessing and a curse: the blessing, if you listen to the commandments of the LORD your God, which I am commanding you today; and the curse, if you do not listen to the commandments of the LORD your God, but turn aside from the way which I am commanding you today, by following other gods which you have not known. (Deut. 11:26–28)

Since that time, Israel's history has been filled with blessings and curses. Obedience has resulted in peace and prosperity; disobedience has resulted in calamity and exile. Yet, such warnings do not negate the unconditional nature of God's promise to Abraham and his descendants.

For example, shortly after my oldest daughter was born and even before our second daughter was born, Amy and I prepared our wills, which leave everything to our children. At the time we drew up our wills, we did not know what our children would be like or even how many children we would have; nevertheless, everything would be equally divided among our offspring upon our deaths.

As our daughters have matured, we have established rules around our house—our own list of "blessings and curses" á la Deuteronomy: "If you perform your chores, you get your allowance; if you talk back to your parents, you forfeit your allowance." Our girls have experienced both blessings and curses under our system of rules. But although their disobedience

might cause them to lose their allowance and experience our
wrath, it never endangered their ultimate inheritance. They are
our children, and no amount of disobedience will cause them to
forfeit their birthright.

In the same way, disobedience to God's law (which came
more than four hundred years *after* God's promise to Abraham)
brought God's severe discipline, but it never endangered the
inheritance of the believing Israelites. The apostle Paul
explained it this way:

> What I am saying is this: the Law, which came
> four hundred and thirty years later, does not
> invalidate a covenant previously ratified by God,
> so as to nullify the promise. For if the inheritance
> is based on law, it is no longer based on a promise;
> but God has granted it to Abraham by means of a
> promise. (Gal. 3:17–18)

The psalmist also understood the difference between
God's conditional and unconditional promises to Israel:

> If his sons forsake My law,
> And do not walk in My judgments,
> If they violate My statutes,
> And do not keep My commandments,
> Then I will visit their transgression with the rod,
> And their iniquity with stripes.
> But I will not break off My lovingkindness from him,
> Nor deal falsely in My faithfulness.
> My covenant I will not violate,
> Nor will I alter the utterance of My lips. (Ps. 89:30–34)

Perhaps the greatest evidence for the unconditional nature of the Abrahamic Covenant is in the ratification of that covenant as recorded in Genesis 15. Abraham understandably wanted assurance that God would do what He had promised to do. So he asked,

> "O Lord God, how may I know that I shall possess it?" So He said to him, "Bring Me a three year old heifer, and a three year old female goat, and a three year old ram, and a turtledove, and a young pigeon." Then he brought all these to Him and cut them in two, and laid each half opposite the other; but he did not cut the birds. (Gen. 15:8–10)

In Abraham's day, whenever two leaders made an agreement with one another, they would cut the animals into two parts along the backbone and place them in two rows, facing each other with a space in between them. Then, the two parties making the covenant would walk together between the animal pieces, signifying the responsibility each party had to keep his part of the agreement. Using this familiar ritual, God ordered Abraham to cut the animals into two pieces, leaving a path between the animals. But then God did something most unusual. Instead of walking with Abraham between the pieces of the animal, God put Abraham to sleep!

> Now when the sun was going down, a deep sleep fell upon Abram; and behold, terror and great darkness fell upon him. (Gen. 15:12)

God, represented by a smoking oven and a flaming torch, then walked through the animal pieces by *Himself:*

And it came about when the sun had set, that it
was very dark, and behold, there appeared a
smoking oven and a flaming torch which passed
between these pieces. On that day the LORD made
a covenant with Abram. (Gen. 15:17–18)

God was demonstrating to Abraham, and to all subsequent generations, that His promise to Abraham was unconditional. This agreement did not depend upon Abraham and his
descendants keeping their end of the bargain. The fulfillment of
this promise rested *solely* on the faithfulness of God. And that is
why Hebrews 6:13 says, "For when God made the promise to
Abraham, since He could swear by no one greater, He swore by
Himself." ·

The Promise Today

What does all of this have to do with understanding Bible
prophecy? God *is* going to fulfill the promise that He made to
Abraham and his believing descendants. Since 1948, Israel has
been occupying a portion of the land God has promised, but it
has never possessed *all* of the land promised to Abraham in
Genesis 15:18–21. Although a descendant of Abraham's (Jesus
Christ) did come to bring a spiritual blessing to the entire
world, the Messiah is not yet ruling over the entire earth as God
later promised to David, Isaiah, and the prophets. To put it
bluntly, God has some unfinished business here on planet Earth.
And the rest of the Bible, from Genesis 12 to Revelation 22, is
the story of God's ultimate fulfillment of His promises to
Abraham and his spiritual descendants.

You may wonder why you should be concerned about God keeping His promise to Israel. What difference does it make to those of us who are not Israelites? The same God who has made unconditional promises to believing Israel has also made unconditional promises to you and to me.

> "And I give eternal life to them, and they shall never perish; and no one shall snatch them out of My hand." (John 10:28)

> Hence, also, He is able to save forever those who draw near to God through Him, since He always lives to make intercession for them. (Heb. 7:25)

> For He Himself has said, "I WILL NEVER DESERT YOU, NOR WILL I EVER FORSAKE YOU." (Heb. 13:5)

How can we know that God will not change His mind and rescind those promises? How can we be sure that when we stand before God He will not say, "I know you were depending on Christ to save you, but I have changed my mind. I am going to judge you by your works instead of grace." Our only hope is that God is a God of integrity who will keep His word. Romans 11:29 promises that "the gifts and the calling of God are irrevocable."

The same God who can be trusted to fulfill His pledge to you will also keep His covenant with Abraham—a covenant that affects not only Israel, but the entire world. And in the subsequent chapters, we will see how God is going to accomplish that.

Getting the Big Picture

I had to learn the value of maps the hard way some years ago. A pastor friend had invited me to Canada to speak at his church's annual Valentine banquet. I departed the Dallas-Ft. Worth airport early one morning and, after a plane change in Minneapolis, landed in Winnipeg around 4:00 that afternoon with plenty of time to spare. After retrieving my luggage, I stood out front waiting . . . waiting . . . and waiting for my host to arrive. After about thirty minutes, I strolled back inside the terminal to call the pastor's home. When I looked at the information letter he had mailed a few weeks earlier, I noticed that the city and province on the letterhead did not correspond to my present location. Because I had preached for the pastor at his church in Winnipeg ten years earlier, I had assumed he was still in the same location.

I took the letter to the airline counter, explaining that I

had apparently traveled to the wrong city. According to the letter, I needed to be in Vancouver, British Columbia. Not knowing much about Canada, I innocently asked, "Is there a bus I can catch to Vancouver? I need to be there in about thirty minutes."

"A *bus?*" All the employees behind the counter exclaimed in unison: "You've got to be kidding! Vancouver is 1,500 miles from here!"

Fortunately, a plane was getting ready to depart for Vancouver in the next few minutes. Even though it was a three-hour flight, the two-hour time change worked to my advantage, and I arrived at the church just in time to preach. As I was boarding the flight that evening, the ticket agent handed me a map of Canada. (Apparently the story of my mistake had already traveled from the ticket counter to the departure gate!) "Here, read this; it might help you next time!" she chuckled. Since then, I have been a firm believer in maps—especially when traveling in a foreign country.

To most people, Bible prophecy is a foreign country. Although many of us have a vague understanding of end-time events (things are supposed to get worse, Jesus is coming back, and Christians will live happily ever after), we would find it difficult to define the major events of Bible prophecy and place them in sequential order. Let's take a moment and test *your* knowledge of end-time events.

See if you can write a one-sentence description of each of the following events as if you were trying to explain it to a friend who had little knowledge of the Bible. (If you find that too easy, then also give a supporting Scripture reference that describes each of these events.)

End-Times Quiz

- The Great White Throne Judgment:

- The Tribulation:

- The Rapture:

- The Millennium:

- The Church Age:

And now for the bonus round, explain the difference between . . .

- premillennialism:

- amillennialism:

- postmillennialism:

- pretribulation rapture:

- midtribulation rapture:

- posttribulation rapture:

Not only would the majority of Christians find it impossible to complete the above quiz; they would also wax eloquently about why such details are unimportant:

- "I'm not on the planning committee for Christ's return; I'm on the welcoming committee."

- "I'm a panmillennialist. Everything will 'pan out' in the end."

- "I don't want to be so heavenly-minded that I'm no earthly good."

Yet, as we have already seen, a basic understanding of the end-time events is both important *and* possible. This chapter will give you an overview and the big picture. We are going to briefly define each of the major end-time events—along with the major supporting Scriptures for each event—according to the *premillennial, pretribulation rapture* view (don't worry, we'll get to all of that later). We will conclude the chapter by briefly looking at how Jesus tied all of these events together in Matthew 24–25.

A Survey of End-Time Events

We are now ready to unfold the map and look at the big picture of end-time events. The following chart shows in sequence the seven major prophetic events that are yet to occur.

1. The Church Age (Rom. 11:25)

Imagine the following situation. You want to give your ten-year-old son a birthday party he will never forget. You purchase an exquisite cake, hire an expensive entertainer, and send out elaborate invitations to your extended family several weeks ahead of time. However, the day before your son's party, every one of your family members calls and sends his regrets. They offer all kinds of flimsy excuses why they cannot attend the gathering. Not wanting to disappoint your son, you quickly begin calling friends, acquaintances, and neighbors, inviting them to attend the party.

Jesus used the above illustration (more or less) to explain the time we are living in now, known as the Church Age (see Matt. 22:2–14). The Church Age is that period of time from Pentecost until the Rapture (a term we will discuss in the next section) during which Gentiles are invited to participate in the blessings of the Abrahamic Covenant. In the Church Age, God has extended the "invitation list" beyond the Jews to include anyone who will accept His offer of salvation.

Since the time of Genesis 12, the story of the Bible is the story of God's dealings with the nation of Israel. Over a period of thousands of years, God has attempted to bring Israel into a right relationship with Himself. Although there are many instances in the Old Testament of non-Jews (Gentiles) being saved, the primary focus has been on Israel. However, after Israel rejected Jesus Christ, God temporarily halted His dealings with Israel and turned His attention toward the Gentiles. The key word here is *temporarily.* In Romans 11, Paul explained that God is not through with Israel. Israel's hardness of heart is only a temporary condition:

I say then, God has not rejected His people, has
He? May it never be! For I too am an Israelite, a
descendant of Abraham, of the tribe of Benjamin.
. . . For I do not want you, brethren, to be unin-
formed of this mystery, lest you be wise in your
own estimation, that a partial hardening has happened to Israel until the fulness of the Gentiles has
come in. (Rom. 11:1, 25)

Because Israel rejected Christ, we who are Gentiles got
invited to the party! Yet God has not permanently turned His
back on Israel. As we saw in the last chapter, God will one day
fulfill His promise to believing Israel of a land, a seed, and a
blessing. God has one final event in mind to turn the Israelites
toward Himself: the Great Tribulation. But before that final
period of dealing with Israel can begin, another event must first
occur.

2. The Rapture of the Church (1 Thess. 4:13–18)

As you can see on the chart, the Church Age will end
with an event many refer to as the Rapture of the Church. The
word *rapture* comes from a Greek word *harpazo,* which means
"to snatch away." That is what the Rapture is—a snatching away
of all believers before the beginning of the Tribulation. The signal passage in the New Testament that describes the Rapture is
1 Thessalonians 4:16–18:

For the Lord Himself will descend from heaven
with a shout, with the voice of the archangel, and
with the trumpet of God; and the dead in Christ

shall rise first. Then we who are alive and remain
shall be caught up together with them in the
clouds to meet the Lord in the air, and thus we
shall always be with the Lord. Therefore comfort
one another with these words.

There are three different views regarding the timing of
the Rapture. Those who believe in a *pretribulation Rapture* teach
that the Rapture will occur before the Great Tribulation; those
who advocate a *posttribulation Rapture* believe that the Rapture
will occur at the end of the Tribulation and will be almost con-
current with the Second Coming of Christ; and still others
believe in a *midtribulation Rapture* that will occur after the first
three and one-half years of the Tribulation. We will discuss the
pros and cons of each viewpoint in the next chapter.

A number of fine evangelical scholars dismiss the whole
idea of a Rapture by raising a number of questions:

- If the Rapture is a reality, why is the term not found in
  the Bible?
- Why did Jesus fail to mention the Rapture of the
  Church?
- Does not a Rapture assume there are three comings of
  Christ instead of two?
- How can anyone believe that the Church will escape
  the suffering of the Tribulation, given the long history
  of suffering by God's people?

We will examine each of these objections in the next
chapter.

3. The Tribulation (Rev. 6–19)

Following the Rapture of the Church is a time commonly referred to as the Tribulation, a seven-year period that begins when the world dictator known as Antichrist signs a peace covenant with Israel and ends with Armageddon and the Second Coming of Jesus Christ. The purpose of the Tribulation is twofold: (1) the redemption of Israel and (2) the condemnation of unbelievers. As we will see in chapter 5, the Old Testament prophets wrote extensively about this future time in Israel's history, referring to it as "the day of the LORD" or the time of "Jacob's trouble." God will severely discipline unbelieving Israel during these years through the world dictator known as Antichrist.

The purpose of God's discipline, however, will be redemptive as evidenced by the conversion of 144,000 Jews at the beginning of the Tribulation. These Jewish converts will serve as missionaries throughout the world during the Tribulation. Although many Jews and Gentiles will be saved through their witness, these converts will pay a heavy price for their conversion. The Tribulation will also be a time for God to pour out His wrath on unbelievers. Three series of judgments (seals, trumpets, and bowls) will result in the deaths of millions and the destruction of a large part of the planet.

If the purposes of the Tribulation are the discipline of Israel and the judgment of unbelievers, what about the Church? What happens to Christians prior to the beginning of the Tribulation? One of the strongest arguments for the pretribulation Rapture (a snatching away of the Church before the Tribulation) is that the Tribulation is designed for Israel and unbelievers, instead of the Church. We will explore this truth more in the next chapter.

4. The Second Coming of Christ (Rev. 19:11–21)

The climax of the Tribulation will occur during the war of Armageddon, during which the major powers of the world will seek to defeat Antichrist and his forces. However, as the world forces prepare to destroy one another, the heavens will suddenly open and all attention will be directed upward as the entire world sees a sight they will never forget:

> And I saw heaven opened; and behold, a white horse; and He who sat upon it is called Faithful and True; and in righteousness He judges and wages war. . . . And the armies which are in heaven, clothed in fine linen, white and clean, were following Him on white horses. And from His mouth comes a sharp sword, so that with it He may smite the nations; and He will rule them with a rod of iron; and He treads the wine press of the fierce wrath of God, the Almighty. And on His robe and on His thigh He has a name written, "KING OF KINGS, AND LORD OF LORDS." (Rev. 19:11, 14–16)

This passage describes the Second Coming of Christ, which is the *visible* return of Jesus Christ to establish His kingdom on earth. Although there are some similarities between the Rapture and the Second Coming, they are two entirely different events. At the Rapture the Lord comes secretly for His children.

41

He appears in the clouds only to His followers, and His feet never touch the earth. However, at the Second Coming believers and unbelievers alike will witness Christ's return to the earth.

5. The Millennium (Rev. 20:1–3)

The Millennium is the thousand-year period of time during which Christ will reign on the earth, fulfilling God's promises to Abraham and his believing descendants. As we saw in the last chapter, God made a literal, eternal, and unconditional promise to Abraham that his descendants would one day possess a specific land and that one of his descendants would rule the entire world. The Old Testament prophets anxiously anticipated this earthly reign of Messiah. For example, consider these familiar words of Isaiah:

> But with righteousness He will judge the poor,
> And decide with fairness for the afflicted of the earth;
> And He will strike the earth with the rod of His mouth,
> And with the breath of His lips He will slay the wicked.
> . . . .
> And the wolf will dwell with the lamb,
> And the leopard will lie down with the kid,
> . . . .
> They will not hurt or destroy in all My holy mountain,
> For the earth will be full of knowledge of the LORD
> As the waters cover the sea. (Isa. 11:4, 6, 9)

As we will see in chapter 7, it is impossible to place these extensive Old Testament prophecies about Christ's rule on the

42

earth in this present age or in eternity. There must be a future time, prior to the new heaven and earth described in Revelation 21–22, when God will fulfill these promises to believing Israel. That time will be the Millennium.

6. The Great White Throne Judgment (Rev. 20:11–15)

Although only Christians will enter into the Millennium (those unbelievers who survive the Tribulation will be judged at the Second Coming of Christ), there will be people born during the Millennium who will choose to follow Satan rather than Christ. Chapter 8 will explain both that people will be born in the Millennium and that many of them will be deceived by Satan. Nevertheless, the Bible teaches that both events will occur and will precipitate God's final judgment of all unbelievers at an event known as the Great White Throne Judgment. Revelation 20 describes this judgment in detail:

> And I saw a great white throne and Him who sat upon it, from whose presence earth and heaven fled away, and no place was found for them. And I saw the dead, the great and the small, standing before the throne, and books were opened; and another book was opened, which is the book of life; and the dead were judged from the things which were written in the books, according to their deeds. And the sea gave up the dead which were in it, and death and Hades gave up the dead which were in them; and they were judged, every

> one of them according to their deeds. . . . And if
> anyone's name was not found written in the book
> of life, he was thrown into the lake of fire.
> (Rev. 20:11–13, 15)

Although we will explain this judgment in much greater
detail in chapter 8, notice several important characteristics of
this judgment. First, the *subjects* of the judgments will be unbelievers. The occupants of Hades (the temporary dwelling place
of unbelievers who die) are the ones who will stand before the
Great White Throne (Rev. 20:14).

The *basis* for their judgments will be their works (Rev.
20:13). Since these unbelievers have refused the grace of Jesus
Christ, they will be judged as they have chosen to be judged,
according to their works.

Finally, the *result* of the judgment will be eternal damnation (Rev. 20:15). Unbelievers will not be simply destroyed, but
they will be sentenced to an eternity of suffering.

7. Eternity Future (Rev. 21–22)

After the Great White Throne Judgment, the present
earth will be destroyed. The apostle Peter wrote of that event in
his second letter:

> But the present heavens and earth by His word
> are being reserved for fire, kept for the day of
> judgment and destruction of ungodly men. . . .
> But the day of the Lord will come like a thief, in
> which the heavens will pass away with a roar and
> the elements will be destroyed with intense heat,

and the earth and its works will be burned up.
(2 Pet. 3:7, 10)

Following the destruction of this present earth will be the unveiling of a new heaven and earth, as witnessed by the apostle John:

> And I saw a new heaven and a new earth; for the first heaven and the first earth passed away, and there is no longer any sea. And I saw the holy city, new Jerusalem, coming down out of heaven from God, made ready as a bride adorned for her husband. And I heard a loud voice from the throne, saying, "Behold, the tabernacle of God is among men, and He shall dwell among them, and they shall be His people, and God Himself shall be among them, and He shall wipe away every tear from their eyes, and there shall no longer be any death; there shall no longer be any mourning, or crying, or pain; the first things have passed away." (Rev. 21:1–4)

It is significant that John saw both a new heaven *and* a new earth. Many Christians have been taught that our eternal home will be in heaven. But as we will see in chapter 10, *earth,* not heaven, will be our final destination. I don't know about you, but I get excited about that truth since floating around on a cloud has never had much appeal to me!

It *Is* Our Business

Do we really need to know about all of these events? Last year as I stood on the Mount of Olives near Jerusalem, I thought about the question the disciples had asked Jesus in that exact location two thousand years earlier. "Tell us, when will these things be, and what will be the sign of Your coming, and of the end of the age" (Matt. 24:3)? Unlike some today who dismiss Bible prophecy as an irrelevant and unintelligible subject, Jesus said it is important to understand end-time events (notice that He devoted two chapters to His answer), and He clearly explained those events. First, He described the Tribulation:

> "For nation will rise against nation, and kingdom against kingdom, and in various places there will be famines and earthquakes. . . .Therefore when you see the ABOMINATION OF DESOLATION which was spoken of through Daniel the prophet, standing in the holy place" (let the reader understand), "then let those who are in Judea flee to the mountains." (Matt. 24:7, 15)

Jesus said the Tribulation would be followed by His return to earth:

> "But immediately after the tribulation of those days THE SUN WILL BE DARKENED, AND THE MOON WILL NOT GIVE ITS LIGHT, AND THE STARS WILL FALL from the sky, and the powers of the heavens will be shaken, and then the sign of the Son of Man will appear in the sky, and then all the tribes of the

earth will mourn, and they will see the SON OF MAN COMING ON THE CLOUDS OF THE SKY with power and great glory." (Matt. 24:29–30)

Then, Jesus described His judgment of unbelievers:

"But when the Son of Man comes in His glory, and all the angels with Him, then He will sit on His glorious throne. And all the nations will be gathered before Him; and He will separate them from one another, as the shepherd separates the sheep from the goats; . . . Then the King will say to those on His right, 'Come, you who are blessed of My Father, inherit the kingdom prepared for you from the foundation of the world. . . .' Then He will also say to those on His left, 'Depart from Me, accursed ones, into the eternal fire which has been prepared for the devil and his angels.'" (Matt. 25:31–32, 34, 41)

Although Jesus said His disciples could not know the date of His return (Matt. 24:36), He never rebuked them for wanting to understand the events surrounding His return. An understanding of Bible prophecy is both important *and* possible, as Matthew 24–25 demonstrates.

But Matthew 24–25 also raises a question. According to Jesus' reply, the next significant prophetic event would be the Tribulation. Why did Jesus fail to mention the Rapture of the Church? Are Christians going to have to endure this time of unparalleled punishment? Before you build a bomb shelter in your backyard and load up on cans of tuna fish and peanut butter, you might want to read the next chapter.

Not
Left
Behind

W hen I was in high school, our English teacher instructed us to present "as creatively as possible" a report on the book of our choice. I chose Hal Lindsey's popular book *The Late Great Planet Earth,* reasoning that my report would be a great witnessing opportunity, especially since our teacher was Jewish. I spent the first thirty minutes of the presentation explaining the events that will precede the Second Coming of Christ, giving particular emphasis to the invasion of Israel by forces from the north, whom Lindsey identified as Russia. This was particularly interesting to our class since, at the time, President Nixon was in Moscow trying to ease tensions with the Soviet Union. What no one in the class knew was that I had prearranged for our assistant principal to interrupt my presentation by coming over the intercom at a designated time with this announcement:

Students and faculty. We have just received word from United Press International that Russia has invaded Israel. President Nixon is returning from Moscow to Washington at this hour. Students and faculty are urged to leave immediately and seek shelter.

My teacher shouted, "Oh, my God! It's true! It's true!" as she and the students raced for the exit. I quickly assured them that it was just part of the presentation, intended to demonstrate how current world events coincided with biblical prophecy.

Unfortunately, instead of piping the announcement into our room only, the assistant principal flipped the wrong switch and the entire school heard the evacuation command, without benefit of my explanation. Suddenly I heard lockers slamming and voices shouting as three thousand people started filing out of the school! Twenty-five years later some of my classmates still remind me of that spring day when it looked as if the world might end. At least I made my point—though my grade on the project did not reflect appropriate appreciation from my teacher (who remained unconvinced and unconverted).

The events that precede the Second Coming of Christ will indeed be terrifying to unbelievers: wars, earthquakes, famine, and economic chaos. Fortunately, Christians will not experience those hardships because of an event that is the focus of this chapter: the Rapture of the Church. Many people do not accept the idea of a snatching away of the Church prior to the Tribulation, but as we view this event in the context of God's prophetic plan, I think you will understand why a Rapture of the Church is essential.

Everyone Loves a Mystery

In chapter 2 we discussed God's promise to Abraham and his descendants of a land, a seed, and a blessing. We saw that this was a plan that was literal, eternal, and unconditional, meaning that one day God will be obligated to fulfill His promise to believing Israel. That is certainly good news for the Jews, but what about the rest of us who are not Jews? How does the Abrahamic Covenant benefit us?

Throughout the Old Testament there were hints—strong hints—that God's blessings would extend to Gentiles also. In the Abrahamic Covenant itself, God promised Abraham that "in you all the families of the earth shall be blessed" (Gen. 12:3). Ruth, Rahab, and the residents of Ninevah are just three examples of Gentiles in the Old Testament who were the beneficiaries of God's grace originally promised to Abraham.

In the New Testament, Jesus also alluded to believing Gentiles receiving God's grace. When Jesus told a story about a king who invited people off the street to attend his son's wedding banquet when the invited guests failed to respond, the Pharisees knew exactly what Jesus was teaching: because of Israel's rejection of Christ, God would allow Gentiles to be fellow-heirs to the promises of God (Matt. 22:1–14). Such an idea was so distasteful to the Jews that when Jesus finished His story "the Pharisees went and counseled together how they might trap Him in what He said" (Matt. 22:15).

Yet, in spite of these strong hints, the Old Testament prophets and the apostles did not fully grasp the idea of Gentiles being recipients of God's promises. This was a "mystery" left to the apostle Paul to explain:

That by revelation there was made known to me
the mystery, as I wrote before in brief. . . . Which
in other generations was not made known to the
sons of men, as it has now been revealed to His
holy apostles and prophets in the Spirit; to be
specific, that the Gentiles are fellow heirs and fellow members of the body, and fellow partakers of
the promise in Christ Jesus through the gospel.
(Eph. 3:3, 5–6)

Whenever we read the word *mystery,* we think of something eerie, like a good Alfred Hitchcock thriller. But the word
translated "mystery" simply refers to something previously hid-
den that has now been revealed. Paul is saying that God gave
him the task to unveil this mystery: that Gentiles would be fellow recipients with the Jews of God's blessings.

What does such a mystery have to do with the Rapture
of the Church? It explains why neither the Old Testament nor
Jesus ever mentioned it. Remember that in the last chapter we
saw that when the disciples asked the Lord about the events
preceding His return, Jesus began with the Tribulation, not the
Rapture. The diagram below details the events explained by
Jesus in Matthew 24–25:

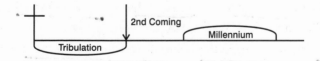

Trust in God.

"Gentile opportunity given

Why is there no mention of a Rapture of the Church by the Old Testament writers or by Jesus? Because the whole idea of a Church Age during which Gentiles would come to faith in Christ was a mystery that the prophets did not fully grasp and Jesus chose not to reveal. Jesus told His Jewish disciples that as far as Israel was concerned, the next event on God's prophetic timetable was a time of tribulation that would end with the return of the Lord and the establishment of His kingdom.

But when Israel rejected Christ, God hit the "stop" button on His prophetic stopwatch. There are seven years remaining on the clock known as the Tribulation during which God will give Israel one last chance to repent. But before those final seven years begin, God is giving Gentiles an opportunity to trust in Christ. This "pause" in God's program is the time we call the Church Age. Look again at Romans 11:25:

> For I do not want you, brethren, to be uninformed
> of this mystery, lest you be wise in your estima-
> tion, that a partial hardening has happened to
> Israel until the fulness of the Gentiles has come in.

Israel's rejection of Christ has caused God to *temporarily* set aside His plans with Israel. However, during this pause in God's dealings with Israel, Gentiles have the opportunity to trust in Christ. We have actually benefited from Israel's rejection of Christ! But when all of the Gentiles who will be saved have been saved, God will hit the "start" button of the stopwatch, and the final seven years of God's dealings with Israel will commence.

Whew! I realize that is a lot of content to digest, so let's take a breather while I tell you a sad story from my love life. Don't worry; it has a happy ending. My wife and I met in Mrs.

Denny's seventh-grade math class when we were twelve years old. It was love at first sight! We started dating in the ninth grade, but when we became sophomores in high school, Amy made what I considered to be a foolish decision: she decided she wanted to date other guys. Her decision broke my heart. As the country-western song says, "She done stomped on my aorta!"

After moping around for several months, I decided to make the most of all the free time I suddenly had. I organized several Bible studies and started spending time with friends who were not yet Christians. One of those friends was a girl in my English class who was very interested in spiritual matters. After several months she prayed to trust in Christ as her Savior. Later that year, Amy and I got back together and have enjoyed a wonderful relationship.

About a year ago, I received a letter from that girl I had led to Christ. She told me all about her spiritual growth and thanked me for the part I had played in God's plan. Then she made this observation: "It's funny, but if Amy had not broken up with you that year, I doubt you would have ever taken the time to share Christ with me."

What a perfect picture of what God has done with the Jews and the Gentiles. Because of Israel's rejection of Christ, the Gentiles have been given an opportunity to believe. But like Amy, Israel's hardness of heart is only temporary. Once the "fulness of the Gentiles" (the Church Age) is complete, God will resume His final time of dealing with Israel. Yet, before that final seven years commences, the Bible teaches that God is going to remove His Church from the earth in the event known as the Rapture.

The Rapture in Scripture

Since Paul is the one to whom God chose to reveal the mystery of the Church Age, it should be no surprise that Paul is also the one who revealed the event that would *end* the Church Age: the Rapture. First Thessalonians 4–5 is the New Testament passage that most clearly outlines the details of this event. Paul wrote this letter to encourage a group of Christians who were discouraged at the Lord's delayed return. They fully believed that Jesus would return in their lifetime. Now that some of their loved ones were beginning to die, they were filled with questions.

- "What will happen to our loved ones who die before the Lord returns? Will they miss out on the resurrection?"

- "What about those of us who are alive when Christ returns? Will we receive our resurrection bodies then or later?"

And so Paul gave this response:

> But we do not want you to be uninformed, brethren, about those who are asleep, that you may not grieve, as do the rest who have no hope. For if we believe that Jesus died and rose again, even so God will bring with Him those who have fallen asleep in Jesus. (1 Thess. 4:13–14)

(A word of explanation about the term *asleep* might be helpful here. Paul used that term to explain what happens to a Christian's *body* at death, not his spirit. The Bible never teaches

54

that a Christian's spirit goes to sleep when he dies. When a believer dies, his or her spirit goes immediately into the presence of Christ. Paul wrote in 2 Corinthians 5:8 that "to be absent from the body" is "to be at home with the Lord." Thus, the term *sleep* refers to the physical body of a Christian. Let's continue.)

> For this we say to you by the word of the Lord, that we who are alive, and remain until the coming of the Lord, shall not precede those who have fallen asleep. For the Lord Himself will descend from heaven with a shout, with the voice of the archangel, and with the trumpet of God; and the dead in Christ shall rise first. Then we who are alive and remain shall be caught up together with them in the clouds to meet the Lord in the air, and thus we shall always be with the Lord. Therefore comfort one another with these words. (1 Thess. 4:15–18)

Notice the four ingredients of the Rapture Paul explained in this passage.

1. The Descent of Christ

The first aspect of the Rapture is the descent of Christ from heaven. "The Lord Himself will descend from heaven" (1 Thess. 4:16). At the Rapture the Lord Jesus Christ will appear to His followers, not on earth, but "in the air" (v. 17). In verse 15, Paul described the Rapture as "the coming of the Lord." The word translated "coming" is the Greek word *parousia,* which is also used in Matthew 24:27 to describe the Second Coming of Christ:

> For just as the lightning comes from the east, and
> flashes even to the west, so shall the coming of the
> Son of Man be.

"Robert, doesn't the fact that the same word is used to describe both the Rapture and the Second Coming prove that they are one and the same?" Not at all. My friend and former professor, Dr. Charles Ryrie, makes a significant point when he reminds us that just because things are similar does not mean they are identical. For example, my car has a motor; my washing machine has a motor; and my automatic camera has a motor. But are these three items identical? Of course not.

Suppose, Dr. Ryrie theorizes, that some proud grandparents say to their friends, "We are looking forward to the coming of our grandchildren next week," and then later in the conversation say, "We are expecting our grandchildren at our golden wedding anniversary." From those two statements you could assume that (a) the grandparents are saying that their anniversary is next week and, thus, are speaking of their grandchildren's arrival and their anniversary as a single event, or (b) the grandparents are referring to two different events. The grandchildren are coming next week for a visit, but they will also be returning at a later time for the anniversary celebration.[1]

The fact that the Lord appears at both the Rapture and the Second Coming does not mean these two events are identical. While there are some similarities between the Rapture and the Second Coming, there are also many differences that we will more fully explore in chapter 6. But one major difference between these events is mentioned in 1 Thessalonians 4:17:

> Then we who are alive and remain shall be caught
> up together with them in the clouds *to meet the*
> *Lord in the air.* (Author emphasis)

At the Rapture, Christ never sets foot on the earth; at the Second Coming, "His feet will stand on the Mount of Olives, which is in front of Jerusalem on the east" (Zech. 14:4). Although Christ will appear in the clouds, the Rapture is not so much about His coming as it is our going!

2. The Resurrection of the Dead in Christ

The second aspect of the Rapture is the resurrection of the physical bodies of the "dead in Christ." When we die, our spirit—the essence of who we really are—goes immediately into the presence of Christ. But our body is left behind, just as the body of Christ remained in the tomb until that first Easter morning. However, our body will not remain in the grave forever. When the trumpet of God sounds, "the dead in Christ shall rise first." The graves will be opened and the bodies of believers will rise toward heaven.

Who are "the dead in Christ" whose bodies will be raised at the Rapture? Some believe they include all believers since the beginning of time—Adam, Eve, Abraham, Moses, David, Ruth, Rahab, and all of the Old Testament saints. However, I believe that the phrase "dead in Christ" refers only to those believers who have died since the ascension of Christ. The Rapture is an event for the Church.

If that is true, then when do these other believers receive their new bodies? We will discuss that issue in chapter 8. But in this passage Paul was addressing Christians who had died in the Church Age. He was comforting those Thessalonians who had lost loved ones by saying, "Death is not as final as it seems. Your loved ones have not missed out on the coming of the Lord. In fact, they will be the first to receive their brand-new bodies."

As I write these words, tears fill my eyes as I think about a little cemetery in Van Alstyne, Texas, where the bodies of my great-grandmother, my grandmother, my grandfather, my mother, and my father are buried. That plot of ground has been the site of some of the saddest moments of my life as I have repeatedly wept over the loss of those people whom I loved most. But one day, Paul said, that place of defeat will become a place of victory when God has the final word.

3. The Removal of All Living Christians

Paul explained that after the resurrection of the "dead in Christ," those Christians who are alive at the time of the Rapture will be suddenly "caught up together with them in the clouds to meet the Lord in the air" (1 Thess. 4:17). This means that there will be a generation of Christians who will never experience death. Their entire being—body, soul, and spirit—will suddenly be removed from the earth, just as Enoch and Elijah in the Old Testament were transported to heaven without ever experiencing death.

One common objection to the idea of a Rapture is that the term is never used in the Bible. If that were true, it would not negate the reality of the Rapture. For example, we believe in the Trinity even though the word *trinity* is never found in the Bible. However, the term *Rapture* is a biblical term. The Latin translation of "caught up" in 1 Thessalonians 4:17 is *rapturo,* from which we derive the English word *Rapture.* The original Greek term *harpazo* is used in the New Testament thirteen times and in two instances describes the physical removal of a person from the earth.

For example, the word is used in Acts 8:39 to describe Philip's supernatural removal from Gaza to Caesarea. The word was also used by Paul in 2 Corinthians 12:2–4 to describe Paul's being caught up into the third heaven. Thus, there is no doubt that Paul was using the word *harpazo* in 1 Thessalonians 4 to describe the physical removal of people from the earth to heaven.[2]

How will the unbelievers explain the disappearance of millions of people from the earth? It is only conjecture, but possibly the Rapture will coincide with some great, international disaster that will signal the beginning of the Tribulation and will be a catalyst for a world dictator who can bring order out of chaos.

4. The Transformation of Our Bodies

Another common question about the Rapture concerns the nature of our new bodies. Specifically, how can deteriorating corpses and even the bodies of living Christians ever enter the kingdom of God? Paul explained this ingredient of the Rapture in 1 Corinthians 15:50–55.

But first, allow me to paraphrase that passage:

> Here's a simple fact of life: You can't enter into heaven in your present bodies. That which is temporal cannot enter that which is eternal.

So what is the solution to this dilemma? Paul said that at the Rapture our bodies will experience a radical transformation:

> Behold, I tell you a mystery; we shall not all sleep, but we shall all be changed, in a moment, in the twinkling of an eye, at the last trumpet; for the trumpet will sound, and the dead will be raised imperishable, and we shall be changed. For this perishable must put on the imperishable, and this mortal must put on immortality. (1 Cor. 15:51–53)

As we saw in 1 Thessalonians 4, not every Christian will die ("sleep"). Those Christians who are alive at the Rapture will not taste death; instead, they will be snatched away into heaven. However, every Christian must experience a transformation of his mortal body into an immortal body ("we shall all be changed"). At the Rapture our bodies, as well as the bodies of those who have already died, will be transformed instantly into the type of body Jesus possessed after His resurrection. In many ways these new bodies will be radically superior to our present bodies; but in other ways, they will be similar to our present bodies. We will explore these similarities and differences in chapter 10.

Last week a viewer of our television program *Pathway to Victory* called with a question: "Dr. Jeffress, I have terminal cancer, and I know that my children cannot afford a funeral. So I have decided to donate my body to a medical school.

However, I found out that once the medical school is finished with my body, they will cremate my remains. Does the Bible condemn cremation?"

I explained to the caller that while Christians traditionally have buried instead of burned their dead, it really does not matter what happens to your physical body after you die. Whether it is lost at sea, burned in a car wreck, blown apart in an airplane accident, or transplanted into someone else's body is irrelevant to God. At the Rapture, God is going to transform the remains of believers into a body that will forever be free of the pain, suffering, and limitations of this life.

The Rapture Question

Throughout history there have been differing views of the Rapture. Since this book is not designed to be a technical treatise on prophecy, I will only briefly summarize the three major views of the Rapture.

1. The Posttribulation Rapture View

Proponents of this position believe that the Church will endure the seven years of the Tribulation. They see the Rapture as separate from the Second Coming, but occurring closely to it. Believers will be caught up with Christ in the air and then return with Christ to earth as described in Revelation 19:14. Advocates of this view argue that it is naive to believe that believers would be exempt from the great suffering described in Revelation 6–19. Furthermore, they observe, the Book of

Revelation describes believers who are present on the earth during the Tribulation and are martyred for their faith. If these believers are not the Church, then who are they?

2. The Midtribulation Rapture View

Others believe that the Rapture will occur after the first three and one-half years of the seven-year Tribulation. They maintain that the first half of the Tribulation, when the Church is still present on earth, will be relatively peaceful. It is only after the first three and one-half years that the world dictator known as Antichrist will break his peace treaty with Israel, ushering in the period of unparalleled persecution of believers that both Daniel and Jesus predicted (see Dan. 9:27 and Matt. 24:15–28). Thus, given the relative peace that will exist during the first half of the Tribulation, there is no need for a Rapture of the Church until the first half is over.

This viewpoint has merit. It is true that Antichrist does not begin his persecution of unbelievers until the final half of the Tribulation. It is also true that the Bible identifies the final half of the Tribulation (forty-two months or 1,260 days) as the time of intense turmoil and persecution (see Dan. 9:27; Rev. 11:2–3; 13:5).

But there are also two major problems with this view. First, it is very difficult to fit all of the events of the Tribulation (discussed in the next chapter) into the final three and one-half years. Although it seems that the majority of judgments will occur in the final half of the Tribulation, some of them appear to begin before then. Second, if the Church is present at the beginning of the seven years of Tribulation, why is there no mention of the Church in Revelation 6–19?

3. The Pretribulation Rapture View

The prefix *pre* means "before." Those of us who believe in a pretribulation Rapture maintain that the Rapture will occur before the beginning of the seven-year Tribulation. I once heard someone say, "I don't know which is the correct view: pre-, mid-, or post-. But I would prefer to be on the first flight going out!" Wouldn't you as well? I am convinced that all Christians are going to be on that "first flight out" because of four key reasons.

1. *The purpose of the Tribulation.* As we have already mentioned, the twofold purpose of the Tribulation is the redemption of Israel and the condemnation of unbelievers. Thus, there is no reason for the Church to be present during the Tribulation.

At our weekly staff meetings, I address the entire staff as a whole about topics that concern all of us. But if I have an issue or problem that needs to be brought to the attention of a smaller group or an individual, I will dismiss the rest of the staff and deal privately with those concerned. Why? Not only for efficiency, but for group morale. I have discovered that no one benefits from a general "bawling out" by the pastor. It is much more effective (and Christian!) to rebuke those needing to be corrected as privately as possible.

The same principle applies to the Tribulation. As we will see in more detail in the next chapter, the purpose of the Tribulation is for the correction of Israel and for the judgment of unbelievers. There is no need for the Church to be on earth for those seven years.

2. *The lack of reference to the Church in Revelation 6-18.* In Revelation 1–5 the Church is prominent. Beginning in Revelation 19 we see the Church returning with Jesus Christ to

earth. But during the description of the Tribulation (Rev. 6–18) there is no mention of the Church. Why? I believe it is because the Church is not present on earth during that horrific period of time.

3. *The teaching of Revelation 3:10.* The Lord told John to write this message to the church at Philadelphia:

> Because you have kept the word of My persever-
> ance, I also will keep you from the hour of testing,
> that hour which is about to come upon the whole
> world, to test those who dwell upon the earth.
> (Rev. 3:10)

The Lord was promising to deliver the Church from (the Greek preposition *ek* means "out of") a universal period of testing "which is about to come upon the whole world." Then, beginning in the next chapter, John began describing that worldwide testing known as the Tribulation. Thus, it is clear that the Lord was promising not only the Church at Philadelphia, but all believers, that they would be delivered "out of" the Tribulation.

4. *The promise of God that believers will be spared His con-*
demnation. Obviously, believers of every age endure times of testing. Jesus told us, "In the world you have tribulation" (John 16:33). Persecution for our faith, sickness, the breakdown of relationships, or just the everyday heartaches that come from living in a sin-infected world guarantee that we will experience suffering. But the distinguishing characteristic of the Tribulation is that it is a time when God will pour out His wrath on an unbelieving world. And God has promised to spare believers from that wrath. Paul wrote,

There is therefore now no condemnation for those
who are in Christ Jesus. (Rom. 8:1)

God took all of the wrath that I deserved and poured it
out on His Son. If I must suffer the wrath of God at some future
time in history, then the death of Jesus Christ was ineffective
and unnecessary. I remember hearing the story of a group of
cowboys who were caught in the middle of a raging prairie fire.
No way of escape was possible. As the fire approached, one of
the men said, "Quick, let's burn the ground around us." At first
the others could not believe such a ludicrous idea until the cow-
boy explained, "The fire cannot come where it has already
been." We are protected from the future wrath of God because
it has already been poured out on His Son. That is the strongest
argument I know for a pretribulation Rapture.

So What?

What does the truth of the Rapture mean to us? The
apostle Paul encouraged Titus to be "looking for the blessed
hope and the appearing of the glory of our great God and
Savior, Christ Jesus" (Titus 2:13). In other words, we should live
with the expectation that at any moment the Rapture could
occur. Although there are numerous prophecies that need to be
fulfilled before the Second Coming, there are *no* prophecies that
must be fulfilled prior to the Rapture. It could happen next year,
next week, or before you finish this chapter. While that truth
does not mean we should quit our jobs, move to a commune,
or max out our credit cards and go to Disney World, we should
live each day with the realization that at any moment the

trumpet could sound, the clouds could part, and the Lord could appear for His own.

Earlier I cited 1 Corinthians 15:52 that speaks of the imminence of the Rapture:

> In a moment, in the twinkling of an eye, at the last trumpet; for the trumpet will sound, and the dead will be raised imperishable, and we shall be changed.

What is the significance of "the last trumpet"? Whenever Roman soldiers were about to break camp and march to a new location, there would always be three blasts of the trumpets. The first blast meant "strike your tents and prepare to depart"; the second blast meant "fall in line"; and the final blast meant "march away."

I believe that God has already sounded the first trumpet. He has reminded us of that need to strike our tents and be living as strangers and aliens in this world that is about to be destroyed. He has also sounded the second blast telling us to be sober and on the alert for His appearance. All we are waiting for is that last blast of the trumpet, at which time we will march away into the presence of our Commander.

When
All Hell
Breaks Loose

*I*n his book *Till Armageddon,* Billy Graham wrote,

The whole world is sighing and suffering on a scale perhaps not known in human history: the refugees, the starving, the "new slaves," the psychological woes, the emotional turmoils, the broken marriages, the rebellious children, the terrorism, the hostages, the wars, and a thousand other troubles which beset every country in the world. There are no people anywhere that are immune. The rich and famous suffer as well as the obscure . . . it seems that the human race may well be heading toward the climax of the tears, hurts, and wounds of all the centuries.[1]

That climax to which Dr. Graham referred is the seven-year period in world history commonly referred to as the Great Tribulation. It will be a time of unprecedented calamity precipitated by political unrest and natural disasters. But the most distinguishing characteristic of this period is that God will pour out His unrelenting wrath upon the inhabitants of the earth. In this chapter we are going to survey the major events of the Great Tribulation. But before we do that, we need to understand God's purpose for the Tribulation. And the place to begin is the Book of Daniel.

God's Man in Babylon

Daniel was a Jewish teenager who was taken captive by the Babylonian king Nebuchadnezzar in the sixth century B.C. The first six chapters of the Book of Daniel record Daniel's remarkable ministry as God's representative during those seventy years of Israel's exile. The final six chapters, however, are prophetic. As you can imagine, Daniel and the Jewish exiles were severely depressed over being uprooted from their homeland and being planted in a strange and pagan culture. These questions must have gone through the Israelites' minds:

- "Has God forgotten the covenant He made with our father Abraham?"

- "Why would God allow a pagan nation to subjugate the people of God?"

- "Will we ever return to our homeland?"

• "Where is that promised Deliverer when we need Him most?"

In response to those questions, God gave Daniel a series of visions that allowed this young prophet/statesman to peer down the corridor of history and see how God would fulfill His promise to His people. After a period of prayer and fasting, Daniel heard this message from the angel Gabriel:

> O Daniel, I have now come forth to give you insight with understanding. At the beginning of your supplications the command was issued, and I have come to tell you, for you are highly esteemed; so give heed to the message and gain understanding of the vision. Seventy weeks have been decreed for your people and your holy city, to finish the transgression, to make an end of sin, to make atonement for iniquity, to bring in everlasting righteousness, to seal up vision and prophecy, and to anoint the most holy place. (Dan. 9:22–24)

As the first portion of Daniel 9 illustrates, Daniel was extremely concerned about Israel's need to return to Jerusalem, so that God's reputation would not be damaged among the Gentile nations. If God was incapable of fulfilling His promise of a secure home for Israel, then He was not a God worthy of worship. Responding to Daniel's sincere concern, God gave the prophet more than he bargained for! In these few verses, God outlined for Daniel His final plan for Israel.

Gabriel announced that there were "seventy weeks" left for God to fulfill His purpose for Israel. The word *weeks* is a poor translation of the Hebrew text. The word can be translated "sevens." Within "seventy sevens," God would complete His earthly plan for Israel. There is ample evidence to support the idea that God is talking about years instead of weeks, especially since earlier in chapter 9 Daniel had been referring to the number of years until Israel's return to Jerusalem (see Dan. 9: 1–2). Thus, I believe that the term "seventy sevens" can be interpreted as seventy weeks of years or 490 years (each week representing seven years). It is the only interpretation that fits the context of this chapter.

Gabriel announced that God would use these 490 years for several purposes:

- "To finish the transgression." This is probably a reference to the end of Israel's rebellion and unbelief.

- "To make an end to sin." This phrase could refer to an end to the sacrificial system.

- "To make atonement for iniquity." I believe this phrase refers to the sacrificial death of Messiah.

- "To bring in everlasting righteousness." This phrase refers to the establishment of Messiah's rule over the earth as prophesied in Isaiah 11.

- "To seal up vision and prophecy." Once Messiah's rule is established, there will no longer be a need for prophecy (or for books on prophecy!).

- "To anoint the most holy place." The "holy place" is obviously a reference to the temple that had been destroyed during the Babylonian invasion. This phrase anticipates a rebuilding of the temple and a reestablishment of the sacrificial system. The question is, which temple? Historically, Zerubbabel rebuilt the temple in 516 B.C. after Israel's return from Babylon. That temple, however, after being enlarged by King Herod, was later destroyed by the Romans in A.D. 70.

As we will soon examine, during the first half of the coming seven-year Tribulation, Israel will once again be offering sacrifices, necessitating the rebuilding of the Temple. Furthermore, sacrifices will be offered during the Millennium, not to atone for sins, but as a memorial to Christ's death, much like the Lord's Supper today commemorates Christ's sacrifice (Ezek. 40:1–46:24 describes the millennial temple and rituals in detail). This will require yet another temple. Thus, this phrase in Daniel may be a reference to Zerubbabel's temple or to some future temple.

Currently there is much talk in Israel about the rebuilding of the Temple. In September 1998, a conference in Jerusalem calling for the rebuilding of the Temple attracted two thousand participants. At the Treasuries of the Temple museum in Jerusalem, one can see a list of projects being undertaken in anticipation of the rebuilding of the Temple, including the creation of the priestly garments as described in Exodus 39.[2]

God's Stopwatch

Obviously, some of these events revealed to Daniel have already been fulfilled, such as Christ's atonement for our sins. Other events are yet to be fulfilled, such as Christ's perfect rule over the earth. Yet Gabriel's message is that all of the events would be fulfilled in a 490-year period of time.

Imagine that God is holding a stopwatch that begins with 490 years. From the time God presses the "start" button until the clock ticks all the way down to "0" years, all of the above described events will take place. That was Gabriel's message to Daniel.

A natural question would be, "When does God press the 'start' button?" Gabriel answered that question in verse 25:

> So you are to know and discern that from the issu-
> ing of a decree to restore and rebuild Jerusalem
> until Messiah the Prince there will be seven weeks
> and sixty-two weeks. (Dan. 9:25)

The 490 years began ticking away, Gabriel said, when-ever the Jews were permitted to leave Babylon and return to rebuild Jerusalem. Although Cyrus authorized the rebuilding of the Temple in 538 B.C., it was the Persian ruler Artaxerxes Longimanus who issued the actual decree to rebuild the city of Jerusalem on March 14, 445 B.C. So on that day, God's final countdown of 490 years began, during which time He would complete His plan for Israel.

Now, here is where it gets really interesting! Gabriel said that from the time that the decree to rebuild Jerusalem was issued until "Messiah the Prince" will be a period of 69 weeks of years (7 weeks + 62 weeks = 69 weeks of years) or 483 years. I believe that the phrase "Messiah the Prince" refers to Jesus' tri-umphal entry into Jerusalem on Palm Sunday, as prophesied in Zechariah 9:9. Thus, Gabriel said 483 years would elapse between the decree to rebuild Jerusalem until the presentation of the Messiah on Palm Sunday. Did that happen?

Dr. J. Dwight Pentecost has demonstrated that exactly 483 years elapsed between those two signal events. Using the Jewish calendar of 360 days, the edict from Artaxerxes was issued on the first of Nisan (March 14, 445 B.C.). Christ rode into Jerusalem on the back of a colt (see Matt. 21:1–11) on the tenth of Nisan (April 2, A.D. 32). Factoring in some of the irregularities of the Jewish calendar, Dr. Pentecost demonstrated that the time between those two signal events was exactly 483 years.[3]

But Gabriel revealed to Daniel that there would be a gap between those first 483 years and the final seven years, during which God will fulfill His plans for Israel:

> Then *after* the sixty-two weeks [plus seven weeks, or sixty-nine weeks] the Messiah will be cut off and have nothing, and the people of the prince who is to come will destroy the city and the sanctuary. And its end will come with a flood; even to the end there will be war; desolations are determined. (Dan. 9:26; Author emphasis)

After Israel rejected Christ and crucified the Messiah, God hit the "pause" button of that imaginary stopwatch. Four hundred and eighty-three years had elapsed; only seven remained. As we saw in the last chapter, this "pause" in God's program with Israel is the time we are living in now: the Church Age. During this time God has *temporarily* turned aside from Israel to allow Gentiles to become heirs of the Abrahamic Covenant. But God is not through with Israel yet. Remember Romans 11:25?

> For I do not want you, brethren, to be uninformed of this mystery, lest you be wise in your

own estimation, that a partial hardening has happened to Israel until the fulness of the Gentiles has come in.

There are still seven years remaining on God's stopwatch. When will those final seven years begin ticking away? Gabriel again provided the answer:

> And he [the great world dictator we call Antichrist] will make a firm covenant with the many for one week, but in the middle of the week he will put a stop to sacrifice and grain offering; and on the wing of abominations will come one who makes desolate, even until a complete destruction, one that is decreed, is poured out on the one who makes desolate. (Dan. 9:27)

The final seven-year countdown will begin with this great world dictator making a peace treaty with the nation of Israel. Halfway through that seven years, this ruler will betray Israel and instigate a period of unparalleled persecution against the people of God. These final three and one-half years, known as the Great Tribulation, will climax with the return of Christ and the establishment of His kingdom.

The Day of the Lord

This seven-year period of time during which God deals with the nation of Israel, as well as the unbelieving world, is known by a variety of titles: "the time of Jacob's distress," "Daniel's seventieth week," "the Great Tribulation." But the most

- Day of the Lord -

common biblical name for this seven-year period is "the day of the Lord." Without exception, the term "day of the Lord" refers to God's judgment against both Israel and the unbelieving world and will culminate in Christ's return and rule over the earth. Look at how some of the Old Testament prophets described the day of the Lord:

> Alas for the day!
> For the day of the LORD is near,
> And it will come as destruction from the Almighty.
> (Joel 1:15)

> Alas, you who are longing for the day of the LORD,
> For what purpose will the day of the LORD be to you?
> It will be darkness and not light;
>
> . . . .
>
> Will not the day of the LORD be darkness instead
>   of light,
> Even gloom with no brightness in it? (Amos 5:18, 20)

> Near is the great day of the LORD,
> Near and coming very quickly,
>
> . . . .
>
> A day of wrath is that day,
> A day of trouble and distress,
> A day of destruction and desolation,
> A day of darkness and gloom,
> A day of clouds and thick darkness. (Zeph. 1:14–15)

The apostle Paul also discussed both the chronology and the characteristics of "the day of the Lord." After explaining the Rapture of the church in 1 Thessalonians 4:13–18, Paul continued by describing the event that will take place after the Rapture: the "day of the Lord":

> Now as to the times and the epochs, brethren, you have no need of anything to be written to you. For you yourselves know full well that the day of the Lord will come just like a thief in the night. While they are saying, "Peace and safety!" then destruction will come upon them suddenly like birth pangs upon a woman with child; and they shall not escape. But you, brethren, are not in darkness, that the day should overtake you like a thief. (1 Thess. 5:1–4)

These four brief verses reveal three important truths about the day of the Lord:

1. The day of the Lord will follow the Rapture of the Church. (1 Thess. 4:13–18)
2. The day of the Lord will be a time of judgment upon unbelievers. (1 Thess. 5:3)
3. Christians need not fear the day of the Lord. (1 Thess. 5:4)

Now that we have seen the reality and purpose of "the day of the Lord," let's look at some of the major events in this seven-year period of time.

Major Events of the Tribulation

The most detailed description of the events of the day of the Lord (or "Great Tribulation") is found in Revelation 6–19. Since it would be impossible to detail this entire period of time in one chapter, allow me to summarize the major events of the Tribulation, using Daniel's division of a beginning, middle, and end.

Act I: The Beginning of the Tribulation

Two major events will characterize the first three and one-half years of the period known as the Tribulation.

A. The Rise of Antichrist

When the 1993 Mideast peace treaty was ratified, one popular radio evangelist announced that the seven years of Tribulation had begun. Obviously, he was wrong, but why did he make such a pronouncement? According to Daniel's outline of this final "week" of years, the signal event that will begin this final period prior to Christ's return will be a peace treaty that Antichrist will make with Israel (Dan. 9:27). I believe that the Rapture of the Church may coincide with some cataclysmic world disaster that will precipitate a universal clamor for a great leader to unite the nations. A disaster such as a nuclear accident, a giant asteroid, a financial meltdown, or another world war could be the catalyst that would set the stage for this great world leader. However, most probably a crisis in the Middle East will bring Antichrist to the world stage.

As I am writing these words, our president has just brokered another peace agreement between Israel and the Palestinians. Even though he has been embroiled in a personal and political scandal, his ability to bring peace to the Middle East has brought him worldwide acclaim. I am not suggesting that our president is the Antichrist, but simply demonstrating how such a future peace treaty with Israel could thrust Antichrist into the political spotlight and provide a platform from which to rule the world.

A combination of verses reveals a number of interesting facts about the Antichrist:

- He will come to power after Christians are removed from the earth, according to 2 Thessalonians 2:6–9 (although it is certainly possible that he could be alive today).

- He most likely will be a Gentile. Revelation 13:1 described him as coming out of the "sea" (a common biblical expression describing Gentiles).

- He will rule over a revived Roman empire that will apparently be in the form of a ten-nation confederacy. Daniel 9:26–27 identifies those who kill Messiah as "the people of the prince who is to come" and as the ones who destroyed the temple—a direct reference to the Romans.

I remember, when I was in high school, hearing the rumor that President John F. Kennedy was still alive, living on some remote island in Greece, and was going to reemerge as the Antichrist. Proponents of this theory pointed to Revelation 13:3:

> And I saw one of his heads as if it had been slain, and his fatal wound was healed. And the whole earth was amazed and followed after the beast.

But I believe a more plausible explanation is that this verse is referring to a political resurrection of the beast's empire (Rome) rather than the physical resurrection of Antichrist himself. The world will be amazed that the Roman empire, thought to be dead, will be resurrected in the form of this ten-nation confederacy presided over by Antichrist.

2. The Rise of the False Prophet

Assisting the rise and rule of Antichrist will be a man, empowered by Satan, commonly referred to as "the false prophet." He will probably be a religious leader who will head a world church described as a "harlot" in Revelation 17. This apostate church will have the appearance of a legitimate church, but will deny the basic tenets of Christianity. Today there are numerous churches that profess belief in the Bible, Jesus Christ, and the Cross. And yet, when you peel away the religious trappings of these churches, you find a belief system that denies the essence of Christianity: that salvation is through faith alone in Christ's sacrificial death.

It will be the same way during the first half of the Tribulation. The false prophet will use his religious influence to promote Antichrist's agenda. However, after the first three and one-half years of the Tribulation, Antichrist will decide that he no longer needs the Church and will destroy it, directing all worship toward himself:

> And the ten horns which you saw, and the beast, these will hate the harlot and will make her desolate and naked, and will eat her flesh and will burn her up with fire. (Rev. 17:16)

After the destruction of this apostate church, the false prophet will move from the religious world to the political world to assist Antichrist in achieving his goals. Specifically, the false prophet will control world commerce by limiting the purchase of goods to those who are willing to demonstrate their allegiance to Antichrist by carrying the number 666:

> And he [the false prophet] causes all, the small and the great, and the rich and the poor, and the free men and the slaves, to be given a mark on their right hand, or on their forehead, and he provides that no one should be able to buy or to sell, except the one who has the mark, either the name of the beast or the number of his name. (Rev. 13:16–17)

The rise of Antichrist and the rise of the false prophet will be the major events of the first three and one-half years of the Tribulation. All indications are that this first half of the Tribulation will be relatively tranquil. "Peace and safety" will be the watchwords of this period (1 Thess. 5:3). Antichrist will be hailed as a hero because he has achieved the unachievable: peace in the Middle East. But halfway through the seven years, Antichrist will do an about-face that will plunge the world into its darkest hour.

Act II: The Midpoint of the Tribulation

The prophet Daniel, the apostle John, and the Lord Jesus Christ all prophesied a key event that would take place halfway through the seven-year tribulation. After the first three and one-half years, Antichrist will break the peace treaty he arranged with Israel and will begin persecuting the Jews, as well as those who will become Christians during that time. Daniel, Matthew, and Revelation all give us great insight into this turning point in the Tribulation.

From the Book of Daniel we learn that this ruler of the revived Roman empire will break his covenant with Israel during the middle of the "week" of years, will become an adversary of Israel, and will make Jerusalem his headquarters during the final three and one-half years of his reign of terror:

> And he will make a firm covenant with the many for one week, but in the middle of the week he will put a stop to sacrifice and grain offering; and on the wing of abominations will come one who makes desolate, even until a complete destruction, one that is decreed, is poured out on the one who makes desolate. (Dan. 9:27)

> I kept looking, and that horn was waging war with the saints and overpowering them. (Dan. 7:21)

> And he will pitch the tents of his royal pavilion between the seas and the beautiful Holy Mountain; yet he will come to his end, and no one will help him. (Dan. 11:45)

The Book of Revelation reveals that the duration of Antichrist's persecution of Israel is three and one-half years (42 months, or 1,260 days):

And leave out the court which is outside the temple, and do not measure it, for it has been given to the nations [Gentiles under the rule of Antichrist]; and they will tread under foot the holy city for forty-two months. (Rev. 11:2)

And I will grant authority to my two witnesses, and they will prophesy for twelve hundred and sixty days, clothed in sackcloth. (Rev. 11:3)

And there was given to him [Antichrist] a mouth speaking arrogant words and blasphemies; and authority to act for forty-two months was given to him. (Rev. 13:5)

Jesus Christ also taught that the last three and one-half years of the Tribulation would begin with Antichrist's turning against Israel and would conclude with His own return to earth:

"Therefore when you see the ABOMINATION OF DESOLATION which was spoken of through Daniel the prophet, standing in the holy place" (let the reader understand), "then let those who are in Judea flee to the mountains; . . . But immediately after the tribulation of those days . . . the sign of the Son of Man will appear in the sky, and then all the tribes of the earth will mourn, and they will see the SON OF MAN COMING ON THE CLOUDS OF THE SKY with power and great glory." (Matt. 24:15–16, 29–30)

Act III: Earth's Final Hours

Jesus described these final three and one-half years as the "great tribulation, such as has not occurred since the beginning of the world until now, nor ever shall. And unless those days had been cut short, no life would have been saved; but for the sake of the elect those days shall be cut short" (Matt. 24:21–22). A study of the different judgments God pours out on the earth during this period of time will help you understand why Jesus would make such a statement. God's judgments against the earth (described in Rev. 6–19) will come in a series of three judgments known as the seal judgments, the trumpet judgments, and the bowl judgments. Space will only allow for a summary of each of these three judgments.

The Seal Judgments

The seal judgments, described in Revelation 6, will begin with the rise of Antichrist (6:1–2) and will include war (6:3–4), famine (6:5–6), death from the famine that will destroy one-fourth of the world's population (6:7–8), martyrdom of those converted after the Rapture of the Church (6:9–11), and tremendous cosmological disturbances (6:12–17). The final seal judgment actually contains all of the trumpet judgments described in Revelation 8:2–11:5.

The Trumpet Judgments

No one can be dogmatic as to whether the seal judgments will occur during the first half or the final half of the Tribulation. Persuasive arguments can be made for either viewpoint. However, when we come to the next series of judgments known as the trumpet judgments, it is evident that we are in the final three and one-half years of the Tribulation.

The first four trumpet judgments are directed against nature, much like the plagues God pronounced upon Egypt during the days of Moses. During the first trumpet judgment, God uses a mixture of hail and fire to destroy one-third of the earth's vegetation (Rev. 8:7). The second trumpet judgment involves "something like a great mountain burning with fire" falling into the sea (Rev. 8:8). Could this be a reference to a giant asteroid? Scientists tell us that sixty-five million years ago a five-mile-wide asteroid struck the Yucatan Peninsula, destroying the dinosaurs. In 1908, a two-hundred-foot rock exploded over Siberia, wiping out thousands of square miles of forest. Today organizations like Spacewatch and Near-Earth Tracking comb the skies for these objects that could one day destroy the planet.[4] Whatever "the great mountain" is, this judgment will destroy one-third of all marine life and one-third of all the ships, resulting in an ecological and economic disaster.

A falling star will destroy one-third of the earth's fresh water supply during the third trumpet judgment (8:10–11). The fourth trumpet judgment will involve a disruption of the rotation pattern of the earth and moon, causing wide fluctuations in temperatures (8:12).

During the fifth trumpet judgment, described in Revelation 9:1–12, Satan (the "star from heaven") will unleash demonic tormentors to persecute mankind, except those who have been sealed by God. These torturers are described as locusts with a sting comparable to scorpions; but their power is derived from Satan. The pain they inflict will be so horrible that people will beg to die, but will be unable to do so (Rev. 9:6). Imagine for a moment the most severe pain you have ever experienced (for me it was a kidney stone). Now, imagine experiencing that pain—without any relief—for five months. That will be the fifth trumpet judgment against the earth.

The sixth trumpet judgment will involve the assembling of a massive army of two hundred million soldiers (Rev. 9:16), who are later described as coming from the east (Rev. 16:12–16). We should probably understand this army as a human army that is demonically empowered by four demons (described as "angels" in Rev. 9:15). The battle described beginning in Revelation 9:18 may be the beginning of the war we refer to as Armageddon, which could extend for several years until the return of Christ.

John noted that this war will kill one-third of mankind (9:18). When you combine this number with those who will already have been killed as a result of the fourth seal judgment (one-fourth of the earth, according to Rev. 6:8), it means that more than one-half of the world's population will have been destroyed. Now we can see why Jesus said that unless these days are cut short no one will survive.

The Bowl Judgments

Like the seventh seal judgment, the seventh trumpet judgment includes all of the next series of judgments: the bowl judgments, as described in Revelation 16:1–21. As we read through these judgments, several facts are obvious. First, they are very similar to the trumpet judgments described in Revelation 8–9. It seems like—to use Yogi Berra's expression—

"déjà vu all over again." But while the trumpet judgments will affect only a portion of the earth, the bowl judgments will impact the entire planet.

The reader of Revelation also can sense the rapidity of these judgments. They probably will occur over the span of just a few days and lead up to the return of Jesus Christ. The final bowl judgment will be especially severe:

> And the seventh angel poured out his bowl upon the air; and a loud voice came out of the temple from the throne, saying, "It is done." And there were flashes of lightning and sounds and peals of thunder; and there was a great earthquake, such as there had not been since man came to be upon the earth, so great an earthquake was it, and so mighty. And the great city was split into three parts, and the cities of the nations fell. And Babylon the great was remembered before God, to give her the cup of the wine of His fierce wrath. (Rev. 16:17–19)

Since this judgment will be poured out "upon the air" and will be accompanied by "flashes of lightning" and "peals of thunder," some have speculated that John was describing a nuclear explosion. If so, it will result in a destruction of Babylon—most likely a reference to whatever city is the seat of Antichrist's power. Babylon was occasionally used as a synonym for Rome in the New Testament (see 1 Pet. 5:13), but could also be a symbol of some other great city such as London, Paris, or Washington D.C. Some have even speculated that John was referring to the actual city of Babylon, which current Iraqi leader

Saddam Hussein has pledged to restore to the splendor of Nebuchadnezzar.[5]

The Sealing of the 144,000

Another important activity during this final three and one-half years of the Tribulation is the calling out of 144,000 missionaries who will be responsible for the conversion of many Jews and Gentiles during the Tribulation. They will be supernaturally sealed and therefore protected by God from destruction by Antichrist. John described a voice from heaven he heard saying,

> "Do not harm the earth or the sea or the trees, until we have sealed the bond-servants of our God on their foreheads." And I heard the number of those who were sealed, one hundred and forty-four thousand sealed from every tribe of the sons of Israel. (Rev. 7:3–4)

Who are these 144,000 individuals who will be supernaturally protected by God during the Tribulation? The Seventh Day Adventists believe it is a reference to their members who are observing the Sabbath when Christ returns. The Jehovah's Witnesses also claim that John had their group in mind here. Christians who believe in a posttribulation Rapture believe the 144,000 represent the Church, which, they believe, will be on earth during the Tribulation.

But such speculation is unnecessary because John clearly identified the 144,000. He explained they will be Jews from each of the twelve tribes of Israel (see Rev. 7:5–8). These Jewish evangelists will be saved after the Rapture and will share the message of Christ with people from every nation. Many Jews and Gentiles will be converted during the Tribulation but will experience great persecution or even death at the hands of Antichrist. After detailing the call of these 144,000 missionaries, John described the result of their ministry: a multitude of converts from every nation who will be martyred by Antichrist:

> After these things I looked, and behold, a great multitude, which no one could count, from every nation and all tribes and peoples and tongues, standing before the throne and before the Lamb, clothed in white robes, and palm branches were in their hands; . . . "These are the ones who come out of the great tribulation and they have washed their robes and made them white in the blood of the Lamb." (Rev. 7:9, 14)

I am often asked this question: "If it is still possible for people to be saved after the Rapture, why not wait until then to see if all of this stuff is really true?" The fact that many will be saved after the Rapture is no excuse for delaying one's decision to trust in Christ. Think about it. If a person is not willing to be saved in this age in which many Christians are spared persecution, why would they be willing to be saved during the Tribulation when they will have to endure tremendous hardships? Nevertheless, some will risk their lives in order to obtain eternal life, which leads to one final word about the Tribulation.

The Purpose of the Tribulation

As I write these words, I am involved in the biggest controversy of my ministry. Because of a stand I have taken in our community against two children's books in our public library promoting the gay agenda, I am being bombarded with media interviews from around the nation. Reporters continue to pose this question: "As a minister, aren't you supposed to be teaching that God is a God of love rather than a God of condemnation?" The inference is that somehow I am being "unloving" by reminding people of God's holiness and intolerance of sin. "Suppose I tell my youngest daughter that if she sticks her finger into an electrical outlet she will die. Am I being judgmental or loving?" I reply. Warning people of the inevitable consequences of sin is the most loving thing we can do, especially if it leads them to make the right choice.

God is perfect love, *and* He is perfect holiness. His holy nature demands that He judge sin, and He will do just that during the Tribulation:

> For behold, the LORD is about to come out from
>   His place
> To punish the inhabitants of the earth for their
>   iniquity. (Isa. 26:21)

But even in the midst of His judgment, we also see God's mercy. If God were simply interested in annihilating unbelievers, why would He dispatch 144,000 missionaries to proclaim His message? Never forget that God's ultimate purpose during these final seven years is to bring Israel, as well as the rest of the world, to a saving relationship with Christ. As God said through the prophet Ezekiel,

"As I live!" declares the Lord GOD, "I take no plea-
sure in the death of the wicked, but rather that the
wicked turn from his way and live. Turn back,
turn back from your evil ways! Why then will you
die, O house of Israel?" (Ezek. 33:11)

What God desires for Israel and the world at large, He
desires for you as well. After writing thousands of pages in his
book on church dogmatics, theologian Karl Barth formulated
this simple definition of God: "the One who loves." Why does
God send tribulation into your life? Because He's angry with
you? Because He likes watching you squirm in discomfort? Of
course not. If God were interested in getting even with you, He
could destroy you with a single word . . . or just a thought. The
Creator of the universe so longs for a relationship with you that
He will use whatever means necessary to drive you into the
arms of the One who loves you.

Here Comes the Bride

*I*n January 1961, a few days before John F. Kennedy was inaugurated as president of the United States, the president-elect invited Billy Graham to spend a day with him in Key Biscayne, Florida. The invitation surprised the evangelist because of Kennedy's well-known dislike for Graham and lack of interest in spiritual matters. After a round of golf, Kennedy and Graham were returning to their hotel when Kennedy stopped the white Lincoln convertible he was driving by the side of the road.

"Billy, do you believe that Jesus Christ is coming back to earth one day?"

"Yes, Mr. President, I certainly do."

"Then why do I hear so little about it?"[1]

The return of Jesus Christ to establish His kingdom is one of the best kept secrets in the world. And yet throughout the Bible we hear the constant refrain that Christ is returning to earth to judge the righteous and the unrighteous.

In this chapter we will examine:

- the events that will precede the Second Coming of Christ,

- the difference between the Rapture and the Second Coming of Christ, and

- the reasons for the Second Coming of Christ.

But first . . . a short review of where we have been.

So Far . . .

In Genesis 12, God promised to Abraham that He would give him and his descendants a specific land, an enduring nation, and a spiritual blessing that would overflow to all the nations of the world. In spite of Israel's continued disobedience, God never wavered in His resolve to fulfill His covenant:

> But I will not break off My lovingkindness from him,
> Nor deal falsely in My faithfulness.
> My covenant I will not violate,
> Nor will I alter the utterance of My lips. (Ps. 89:33–34)

When would God's promises to Israel be fulfilled? This question was particularly relevant to the Israelites who had been exiled to Babylon in 586 B.C. Uprooted from their homeland, these Israelites began to wonder if God had revoked His covenant with them. To reassure the Israelites of His faithfulness, God gave Daniel four visions concerning Israel's future. In the most remarkable vision, God actually specified a timetable for fulfilling His promises to the Israelites. From the time Israel returned to Jerusalem to rebuild the city until God's plan for Israel was completed would be a period of 490 years (Dan. 9:24–27).

However, God also revealed to Daniel that there would be a gap between the first 483 years and the final seven years (Dan. 9:26–27). During that pause, in which we are now living, the apostle Paul explained that God is allowing Gentiles to be saved (Rom. 11:25). But this pause should not be confused with a period. God is not yet finished with Israel; there are seven remaining years left on God's stopwatch. Before this final seven years begins, He is going to remove His Church (those who are saved during this present time period) from the earth in an event known as the Rapture (1 Thess. 4:13–18).

The final seven years of God's plan for Israel is called the Tribulation. As we saw in the last chapter, God's purpose for the Tribulation is twofold: (1) to pour out His wrath on unbelievers and (2) to give unbelieving Israelites and Gentiles one last chance to repent prior to the return of Christ.

While the first three and one-half years of the Tribulation will be relatively peaceful, the final half will be marked by Antichrist's reign of terror upon the earth. But Antichrist will not be the only disruptive force in the world during these final years; God will also be pouring out His wrath in a series of judgments directed against the earth's resources and population.

You've probably heard the old saying, "He who calls the shots, takes the shots." That maxim will also apply to Antichrist. Tired of his tyrannical rule that has resulted in worldwide destruction, leaders of other nations will marshal their forces to challenge Antichrist in a battle known as Armageddon.

Look Up and Look Out

The setting for Armageddon is found in Revelation 16:

> And I saw coming out of the mouth of the dragon and out of the mouth of the beast and out of the mouth of the false prophet, three unclean spirits like frogs; for they are spirits of demons, performing signs, which go out to the kings of the whole world, to gather them together for the war of the great day of God, the Almighty. . . . And they gathered them together to the place which in Hebrew is called Har-Magedon. (Rev. 16:13–14, 16)

While there are many unanswered questions about this climactic world conflict we call Armageddon, John clearly stated that evil spirits proceeding from the Satanic trinity (the dragon = Satan; the beast = Antichrist; and, the false prophet = Antichrist's lieutenant) will lure the armies of the world to this area in Israel known as the Mount of Megiddo or Armageddon. From Antichrist's perspective, he will have a better chance of defeating his numerous enemies if he can contain them in a single location.

My former pastor, Dr. W. A. Criswell, told me once about being on an airplane seated next to the chief of staff at the Pentagon. At that time Dr. Criswell was preaching on the subject of Armageddon, so he asked the chief of staff if he thought it was ever likely that foot soldiers would be outdated and replaced by modern weapons of warfare (Revelation describes infantrymen and horses). The general answered: "Never. We will always need soldiers to push our enemies together. Atomic weapons and hydrogen bombs are of no use if the enemy is deployed over the face of a continent. The only way that an atomic bomb is useful is when we have a concentration of the enemy so you can drop it on them. But in order to push those enemies together, we must have an army to compress them." So it will be at the final world battle known as Armageddon.

One other thought. Although Revelation 16:13–14 says that evil spirits will lure the world forces to Armageddon, God is the ultimate cause of their gathering. First Kings 22 describes how God used an evil spirit to tempt Ahab to wage war against the city of Ramoth-gilead and suffer defeat. God will again employ evil spirits to accomplish the same purpose at Armageddon.

Possibly, like me, you have had the opportunity of standing on the Mount of Megiddo and looking out on this spectacular plain that was the site of many Old Testament battles such as Barak and the Canaanites and Gideon against the Midianites. The plain is fourteen miles wide and twenty miles long. Napoleon called it "the most natural battlefield in the whole earth." Yet, as large as the area is, it is obviously not large enough to contain the number of forces described in Revelation . . . and it doesn't need to. This final world conflict will be waged up and down the entire length of Israel:

> And the wine press was trodden outside the city, and blood came out from the wine press, up to the horses' bridles, for a distance of two hundred miles. (Rev. 14:20)

But it is while the world forces are waging war against one another that God will release His final judgment against the earth:

> And the seventh angel poured out his bowl upon the air; and a loud voice came out of the temple from the throne, saying, "It is done." (Rev. 16:17)

One factor that differentiates this judgment from the preceding ones described in the last chapter is that it will be released "upon the air" instead of on the earth. Could this be a description of some great nuclear explosion? The following verses certainly indicate something of that magnitude.

> And there were flashes of lightning and sounds and peals of thunder; and there was a great earthquake, such as there had not been since man came to be upon the earth, so great an earthquake was it, and so mighty. And the great city was split into three parts, and the cities of the nations fell. And Babylon the great was remembered before God, to give her the cup of the wine of His fierce wrath. And every island fled away, and the mountains were not found. (Rev. 16:18–20)

But this catastrophic judgment against the earth will be merely a prelude to the most dramatic event in human history, the return of Jesus Christ.

Here Comes the King

After a brief interlude during which the apostle John gave further details concerning Babylon, he returned to the climax of the battle of Armageddon. As the world forces are battling Antichrist, suddenly the heavens will open and the armies will drop their weapons as they stare into the sky in stunned silence:

> And I saw heaven opened; and behold, a white horse, and He who sat upon it is called Faithful and True; and in righteousness He judges and wages war. . . . And He is clothed with a robe dipped in blood; and His name is called The Word of God. And the armies which are in heaven, clothed in fine linen, white and clean, were following Him on white horses. And from His mouth comes a sharp sword, so that with it He may smite the nations; and He will rule them with a rod of iron; and He treads the wine press of the fierce wrath of God, the Almighty. (Rev. 19:11, 13–15)

It is obvious that the rider of the white horse is the Lord Jesus Christ. But who are the "armies which are in heaven"? That's you and me! How do I know that? Because earlier in Revelation 19, John described what will be happening in heaven just prior to Christ's return to earth. Christians will be in heaven, preparing to return to earth with the Lord to enjoy the Marriage Supper of the Lamb, a celebration that will occur when Christ returns to establish His kingdom on the earth.

How do you dress for a wedding? As a pastor, I have seen a few people come to a wedding dressed in blue jeans and a

T-shirt, but most people prefer something a little more formal. As believers prepare for the wedding supper with Jesus Christ, we, too, will dress in our best:

> And it was given to her to clothe herself in fine linen, bright and clean; for the fine linen is the righteous acts of the saints. (Rev. 19:8)

When we return to earth with Christ for this celebration, we will not be wearing Hickey Freeman suits or Chanel dresses, but our garments will be related to the righteous deeds we have performed as believers. Before we trust in Christ as our Savior, our good works are worthless before God. The best we can do, Isaiah the prophet said, is like a filthy rag to God. We are saved only by God's grace. Nevertheless, after we become a Christian, good works are vitally important and will determine what kind of eternity we experience (we will discuss this further in chapter 9).

The armies that will return to earth with Christ are described as being dressed "in fine linen, white and clean" (Rev. 19:14) which clearly identifies them as those of us who already will be in heaven. The world forces that are understandably startled by the appearance of Christ and His followers descending from heaven will regain their composure and actually unite to fight Christ and His army:

> And I saw the beast and the kings of the earth and their armies, assembled to make war against Him who sat upon the horse, and against His army. (Rev. 19:19)

In the past I have heard preachers and teachers describe Christians as some type of heavenly "Rambos," charging forward on horseback as they flail their swords and slaughter the forces of Satan. Such a scene might appeal to some testosterone-charged men, but most women wince at such a thought. And people like me who have ridden a horse only twice (and fallen off each time) are more than a little concerned about handling a horse *and* a sword at the same time.

If you share those concerns, don't worry. Contrary to such popular descriptions, the Lord will not need our assistance in winning this battle. He will be able to defeat the armies of the world without lifting a finger:

> And from His mouth comes a sharp sword, so that
> with it He may smite the nations; and He will rule
> them with a rod of iron; and He treads the wine
> press of the fierce wrath of God, the Almighty. . . .
> And the rest were killed with the sword which
> came from the mouth of Him who sat upon the
> horse, and all the birds were filled with their flesh.
> (Rev. 19:15, 21)

Just as God destroyed an army of 185,000 Assyrians in an instant (see 2 Kings 19:35), the same God will slay the armies of the earth with the sharp sword of His Word.

One or Two Comings?

Before we look at the three distinct purposes for Christ's visible return to earth, it might be helpful to explain both the similarities and the differences between the Rapture of the Church (described in chapter 4) and the Second Coming of

Jesus Christ, prophesied throughout the Old Testament and described in Revelation 19. Those who believe in a posttribulation Rapture (see chapter 4) view the Rapture and the Second Coming of Christ as *practically* a single event, occurring after the Tribulation. But those who advocate a pretribulation Rapture of the Church believe that the Rapture and the Second Coming are two distinct events, separated by the seven years of Tribulation.

One reason some people believe that the Rapture and the Second Coming are synonymous is because the Bible uses the same words to describe both events:

- *parousia* (which means "coming," "arrival," or "presence" and is found in 1 Thess. 4:15 and Matt. 24:27);
- *apokalupsis* (which means "revelation" and is used in 1 Cor. 1:7 and 2 Thess. 1:7); and
- *epiphaneia* (which means "manifestation" and is used in 2 Tim. 4:8 and 2 Thess. 2:8).[2]

Each of these words is used to describe both the Rapture and Second Coming of Christ. So isn't it natural to assume that these are both the same events?

In chapter 4 we saw that things can have common elements yet still be quite different. Both my wife and my eldest daughter possess eyes, ears, noses, the same coloring, and warm personalities. They are similar in many ways, but no one would argue they are the same people! The same truth applies to the Rapture and the Second Coming of Christ. In both events there will be a coming of the Lord from heaven (*paraousia*), a revealing of His glory as the Son of God (*apokalupsis*), and a visible manifestation of Himself (*epiphaneia*).

But there are also some major differences between the Rapture and the Second Coming that deserve our attention. First, many prophecies must be fulfilled prior to the Second Coming of Christ, including the return of Israel to her homeland, the rebuilding of the Temple, and the events of the Great Tribulation described in Revelation 6–19. However, no prophecies must be fulfilled before the Rapture of the Church. At any moment, the trumpet could sound and believers could be caught up to meet the Lord in the air. That is why we say that the Rapture is "imminent"—it could happen at any moment. Since many of the prophecies concerning the Second Coming have already been fulfilled (such as Israel's returning to her homeland), the Rapture, which occurs seven years *earlier*, may be closer than ever before.

Another difference between the Rapture and the Second Coming involves the Lord's final destination. At the Rapture, Christ's feet will never touch the earth. Instead, He will appear "in the air" (1 Thess. 4:17) to meet believers. But at the Second Coming, the Lord's feet will touch the earth, and when they do, what a topological reaction there will be! I stood recently on the Mount of Olives and read this verse to our tour group, which describes what will happen at the Second Coming:

> And in that day His feet will stand on the Mount of Olives, which is in front of Jerusalem on the east; and the Mount of Olives will be split in its middle from east to west by a very large valley, so that half of the mountain will move toward the north and the other half toward the south. (Zech. 14:4)

Third, after the Rapture, Jesus will return to heaven with His believers. But at the Second Coming, Jesus will return to earth *with* believers to establish His kingdom.

Fourth, the Rapture is a mystery that is never mentioned in the Old Testament and only involves the Church. But the Second Coming is predicted many times in the Old Testament since it involves God's plan for Israel and the world.

Fifth, after the Rapture, believers only will be judged at the *bema* judgment (we will discuss this judgment in detail in chapter 9). The result of this judgment will determine rewards in heaven. After the Second Coming, Israel and Gentile nations will be judged. The result of their judgment will determine their eternal destiny.

Sixth, after the Rapture there will be no physical change in the earth. But after the Second Coming, part of the curse against the earth will be removed, and the planet will enjoy a partial renovation.

Seventh, after the Rapture, Satan's power will be unleashed on earth for seven years. After the Second Coming, Satan will be bound for a thousand years.

Eighth, the Rapture will occur instantaneously ("in the twinkling of an eye"), but the Second Coming will be the climax of a worldwide conflict involving millions of people.

Finally, at the Rapture only believers will see the Lord Jesus Christ. But at the Second Coming unbelievers will "look on [Him] whom they have pierced" (Zech. 12:10) and "EVERY KNEE [SHALL] BOW and . . . every tongue [shall] confess that Jesus Christ is Lord, to the glory of God the Father" (Phil. 2:10–11).

Why a Second Coming?

Why is a literal, physical return of Jesus Christ to the earth really important? When my wife and I were in high school, she attended a liberal church whose pastor denounced the basic tenets of the Christian faith: the deity of Christ, the substitutionary death of Christ for our sins, the existence of heaven and hell, and the Second Coming of Christ. One Easter Sunday morning I was driving down the highway in my blue Volkswagen Bug on the way to church. That morning Billy Graham was scheduled to speak to our congregation. His topic? The Second Coming of Jesus Christ. As I eagerly anticipated his message, I decided to turn on the radio and listen to the sermon my future wife was hearing in her church. Coincidentally, her pastor was also preaching on the Second Coming, but with quite a different twist. I will never forget what I heard him say.

"For two thousand years people have believed that Jesus Christ is coming back to earth to set up some kingdom. And yet, He hasn't come. And He *isn't* coming either. The first time Jesus came to earth was at Bethlehem. But His Second Coming is when He comes into your heart." The pastor's words were almost identical to the warning of the apostle Peter, who described the taunting by unbelievers in the last days:

> Know this first of all, that in the last days mockers will come with their mocking, following after their own lusts, and saying, "Where is the promise of His coming? For ever since the fathers fell asleep, all continues just as it was from the beginning of creation." . . . But do not let this one fact escape

your notice, beloved, that with the Lord one day
is as a thousand years, and a thousand years as
one day. The Lord is not slow about His promise,
as some count slowness, but is patient toward
you, not wishing for any to perish but for all to
come to repentance. (2 Pet. 3:3–4, 8–9)

The Lord is returning to earth for at least three important purposes. First, He is coming to complete the prophecies of the Bible. There are hundreds of prophecies in both the Old and New Testaments concerning the Lord's return to earth that demand fulfillment. If those prophecies are not fulfilled, then all of God's Word is suspect.

Second, Christ is coming to judge unbelievers. Again, both the Old and New Testaments promise that one day the Lord is going to judge the ungodly:

And He will strike the earth with the rod of His
mouth,
And with the breath of His lips He will slay the
wicked. (Isa. 11:4b)

But the present heavens and earth by His word are
being reserved for fire, kept for the day of judgment and destruction of ungodly men. (2 Pet. 3:7)

Although a number of unbelievers will be killed during the Tribulation, many will survive and must be judged by Christ before He begins His rule upon the earth (to be discussed further in the next chapter).

Finally Christ is coming to reclaim the earth, which was lost to Satan (1 Cor. 15:24–28). If believers are simply caught up in the air to live with Christ in heaven forever, then Satan has been successful in usurping God's creation. Do you believe that God is going to say, "Satan, you won. You can have the earth, and I'll take heaven. You stay in your corner of the universe, and I'll stay in mine." Not on your life!

A seminary student was leaving the school gymnasium after a game of basketball with several friends. As he left, he was surprised to discover a janitor sitting in the bleachers, reading the Book of Revelation. Thinking of his own study of the book in a New Testament class, he asked the uneducated janitor if he understood that complex book of the Bible. "Oh yes, I understand it. It means that Jesus is gonna win."[3]

The Second Coming of Jesus Christ means that Jesus is going to reclaim what is rightfully His. Jesus is going to win . . . and so are we!

Heaven on Earth

Several years ago a mother wrote to "Dear Abby," questioning the goodness of God. In 1988, the woman's beautiful twenty-two-year-old daughter was killed by a drunk driver. The mother got on her knees and pleaded with God to bring her daughter back to life. "You can do anything. You can perform miracles. . . . Please God, let me trade places with her—please let me lie in that coffin, and let her out to live her life." God refused to honor her request. At times, the mother confessed, she had thoughts of suicide but lacked the "courage" to pull the trigger or take the pill that would end her relentless pain. Meanwhile, the drunk driver who killed the girl spent less than six months behind bars. "Today, he walks in the sun while my little girl is in a dark grave."

The mother closed her letter by saying, "God didn't answer my prayers, and I resent being told that I have no right

106

to question God. If there is a God, and if I ever get to meet Him face-to-face, you can bet your life I will have plenty of whys for him to answer. I want to know why my little girl died and that drunk was allowed to go on living. I love her more than my life, and I miss her so. I am mad that I am having to live in a world where she no longer lives. I want to know why . . . I don't fear the Lord. And I don't fear hell, either. I know what hell is like. I've already been there since the day my precious daughter was killed."[1]

Although we might wince at that mother's defiant attitude toward her Creator, we can empathize with her questions. If there is a God, why does He allow murderers to run free, babies to be sexually abused, hundreds of millions around the globe to starve to death? Why doesn't He create a world that is free from injustice, conflict, suffering, and death?

We know from Genesis 1–2 that such a world once existed, until sin caused that paradise to be temporarily lost to Satan's domain. But it has not been lost forever. The most prominent prophetic promise in the Bible is that one day Jesus Christ is going to return to earth and establish a world order that is characterized by perfect peace, justice, and freedom from suffering. That period in history is called the Millennium, and it is the focus of this chapter.

The Millennium in Perspective

Next to the Rapture, the Millennium is the most hotly debated aspect of Bible prophecy. You have probably heard the terms *premillennial, postmillennial,* and *amillennial* (terms we will later explain in detail) and wondered what all the fuss is about. The question is simple, but crucial: "Is Jesus Christ going to return to earth and establish His kingdom on earth?" How you answer that question not only affects your understanding of the future, but it also impacts how you interpret many of the prophecies concerning the kingdom of God found in the Old and New Testament.

The word *Millennium* comes from two Latin words *milli* (meaning "thousand") and *annum* (meaning "year"). Although the word *Millennium* is not found in Scripture, the concept is clearly taught throughout the Bible, including Revelation 20.

Let's first set the scene for Revelation 20. We are at the end of the seven-year period known as the Tribulation. The climax of the Tribulation is the battle known as Armageddon in which the world forces wage war against the great dictator known as Antichrist. In the midst of that battle, the heavens will suddenly part, and Christ will return to earth with His followers. John described the fate of Antichrist and his assistant known as the false prophet:

> And the beast was seized, and with him the false
> prophet who performed the signs in his presence,
> by which he deceived those who had received the
> mark of the beast and those who worshiped his
> image; these two were thrown alive into the lake
> of fire which burns with brimstone. (Rev. 19:20)

But what about the power behind Antichrist and the false prophet? What happens to Satan when Christ returns? John answered that question beginning in chapter 20:

And I saw an angel coming down from heaven, having the key of the abyss and a great chain in his hand. And he laid hold of the dragon, the serpent of old, who is the devil and Satan, and bound him for a thousand years, and threw him into the abyss, and shut it and sealed it over him, so that he should not deceive the nations any longer, until the thousand years were completed; after these things he must be released for a short time. And I saw thrones, and they sat upon them, and judgment was given to them. And I saw the souls of those who had been beheaded because of the testimony of Jesus and because of the word of God, and those who had not worshiped the beast or his image, and had not received the mark upon their forehead and upon their hand; and they came to life and reigned with Christ for a thousand years. The rest of the dead did not come to life until the thousand years were completed. This is the first resurrection. Blessed and holy is the one who has a part in the first resurrection; over these the second death has no power, but they will be priests of God and of Christ and will reign with Him for a thousand years. (Rev. 20:1–6)

Later we will look at some of the characteristics of the Millennium that John mentioned in this passage, but for now I want you to notice the repetition of the phrase "thousand years" in this paragraph. It is found not just once or twice, but five times in six verses! Why is that significant? Suppose you were to send a letter to your brother saying, "The day after Christmas I would like to come and stay at your house for thirteen days. For thirteen days I will enjoy visiting with you and your family. If thirteen days is too long, please let me know." You arrive at your brother's house the day after Christmas, just as you promised. You enjoy several delightful days together. However, on the third day, your brother informs you that he is leaving on a ski trip for two weeks.

"I thought you understood that I would be staying with you for thirteen days."

"I am so sorry," he replies. "I didn't think you actually *meant* thirteen days; I thought you were speaking figuratively."

Figuratively? How could you have been more clear? You didn't say you were going to stay "for awhile" or "until after the first of the year." You were very specific—thirteen days. I wonder if the Lord doesn't experience some of that same frustration when He hears well-meaning Christians trying to interpret Revelation 20.

- "I wonder how long Christ is really going to rule on the earth?"

- "I wonder what John means by 'the earth'?"

- "I wonder if the binding of Satan should be taken figuratively or literally?"

Assume for just a moment that Jesus Christ was going to return to earth and rule for one thousand years. How would John communicate that truth? He would use the very same words we find in Revelation 20. A thousand years means a thousand years. As someone wisely suggested about interpreting the

Bible, "When the plain sense makes good sense, seek no other sense."

Pre-, Post-, or A-?

Throughout history Christians have held various views concerning the nature and the timing of the Millennium. Specifically, the question is, "When is the Second Coming of Christ in relation to the Millennium?"

The premillennial position (the view espoused in this book) is that the Second Coming of Christ occurs prior to ("pre-") the Millennium. But the premillennial position is more than a question of timing. Premillennialists believe in a literal fulfillment of the Abrahamic Covenant we examined in chapter 2. They believe that one day believing Israel is going to inhabit all of the land promised to Abraham, that Jesus Christ is going to rule from the throne of David in the city of Jerusalem, and that Satan will be bound for one thousand years.

Premillennialists also see a distinction between the Church (believers saved between Pentecost and the Rapture) and Israel. Although there are benefits from the Abrahamic Covenant that will extend to the Church during the Millennium, there are other benefits that are peculiar to believing Israel. Since God made an unconditional promise to Abraham and his believing descendants, God is obligated to keep those promises. The Millennium will be that period in history when God will fulfill His promises to believing Israel.

Although some people have tried to distinguish between *historic premillennialism* and *dispensational premillennialism*, the reader should understand that such distinctions are dubious at best. Popular teacher and author Dr. Charles Ryrie wrote,

> Opponents of the premillennial system have attempted to obscure the main issues involved by inventing distinctions between historic premillennialists, pretribulationalists, dispensationalists, and ultra-dispensationalists. Such distinctions are not warranted since the differences involved are so minor and since the roots of premillennialism go far deeper.[2]

The "roots" of premillennialism include the timing of the Millennium (prior to the return of Christ) and the nature of the Millennium (a literal fulfillment of the Abrahamic Covenant).

Postmillennialists believe that Christ will return after ("post-") the Millennium. Proponents of this view believe that the entire world will be evangelized, bringing about the peace and righteousness that will characterize the Kingdom Age. Postmillennialism thrived from the seventeenth century until the middle of the twentieth century. However, two world wars nearly extinguished this belief that the planet was going to get better and better until Christ returned.

Although classical postmillennialism is a minority view, there is a variation of it known as *reconstructionism,* which is very popular today. Christian reconstructionists advocate believers using the political process to bring about the "kingdom of God" here on earth. If we can elect the right individuals into office and legislate Christian reforms, then we can experience the kingdom rule of Christ, the reconstructionist believes. Last year our church was involved in a nationally publicized controversy over the removal of two pro-homosexual children's books in our public library. Our argument was that tax dollars should not be used to support such blatant propaganda targeted toward children. We asked the city council to pass a resolution that would prohibit the purchase of such books in the future. However, regardless of what the city council eventually does, we are not under the illusion that such actions are going to "Christianize" our city or our nation. We do not believe that we are going to legislate the Millennium into existence. We are simply trying to prevent the premature deterioration of our culture.

The real debate in eschatology (the study of the end times) is between premillennialism and amillennialism. The word *amillennial* means "no millennium." Now I must confess to you (if you haven't already figured this out by reading my biographical sketch on the back cover) that I come from a strong premillennial background. Between sitting under the preaching of W. A. Criswell for thirty years and attending Dallas Theological Seminary for four years, I didn't have a chance! But in their zeal to defend the premillennial belief system, I have heard some premillennialists level some unfair charges against amillennialists. "Those infidels don't even believe the Bible. How can they not believe in a Millennium when it is so clearly taught in the Bible?"

The truth is that amillennialists do believe in a Millennium—of sorts. The Millennium they describe is not physical, but spiritual; it is not earthly, but heavenly. Amillennialists interpret the thousand-year reign of Christ described in Revelation 20 as descriptive of Christ's rule in the hearts of His followers that began after the Resurrection and will extend until the Second Coming. At that time, Christ will return to earth, judge the wicked, reward the righteous, and we will enter into eternity. Some amillennialists claim that, although God did make certain promises to Israel in the Old Testament, the Israelites forfeited those unfulfilled promises when they rejected Christ. The promises that were intended for Israel are now reserved for the Church. Furthermore, these promises have been transformed from the physical to the spiritual. Thus, the hope of Israel one day inheriting the promised land has now been transformed into the Church's inheriting heaven.

What about the description in Revelation 20 of the binding of Satan for a thousand years? Amillennialists claim that Jesus Christ has already bound the power of Satan through several actions: (1) resisting him in the wilderness, (2) paying for man's sin at the cross, and (3) destroying the power of death at the Resurrection. Thus, Christians are experiencing the Millennium now to the extent that they allow Christ to rule in their hearts.

I must admit that there is one aspect of amillennialism that is appealing to me: its simplicity! You don't need any complicated charts to explain the end times from the amillennial viewpoint. The final events are simple: Second Coming, judgments, and eternity. No separate Rapture, no complicated judgments, and no distinction between Israel and the Church.

A few years ago I assisted our denomination in writing Sunday school curriculum on Revelation. I was designated as the premillennial representative and another fellow was the amillennial representative. We were scheduled to meet for two days and explain each chapter of Revelation from our particular viewpoints. I spent days preparing my material and arrived with charts, papers, and several stacks of books. My amillennial colleague strolled into the room with nothing except a pocket-sized New Testament! Our discussion leader would ask, "Robert, what is the premillennial view of the seven seals in Revelation 6?" I would launch into a detailed explanation while everyone's eyes glazed over. My amillennial friend would answer, "Probably symbolic." And so it went through most of the two days. In fact, I was so exhausted by the end of our seminar, I was about ready to convert to amillennialism myself. It is *so* much easier!

Although amillennialism has been the most popular millennial view throughout Church history, I believe it has some serious problems, chief of which is the Abrahamic Covenant (see chapter 2). God's covenant with Abraham and his descendants was an unconditional promise, not based on Israel's faithfulness, but on the faithfulness of God. Although Israel would certainly suffer for rebellion against God, He promised never to abandon His covenant with Israel. Remember Psalm 89?

> If his sons forsake My law,
> And do not walk in My judgments,
> If they violate My statutes,
> And do not keep My commandments,
> Then I will visit their transgression with the rod,
> And their iniquity with stripes.
> But I will not break off My lovingkindness from him,
> Nor deal falsely in My faithfulness.
> My covenant I will not violate,
> Nor will I alter the utterance of My lips.
> Once I have sworn by My holiness;
> I will not lie to David.

His descendants shall endure forever,
And his throne as the sun before Me. (Ps. 89:30–36)

The unconditional nature of the Abrahamic Covenant is the main reason I believe that Christians can look forward to a coming kingdom of Christ on this earth. Such a kingdom was prophesied in the Old Testament, anticipated in the Gospels and epistles, and fulfilled in the Revelation.

Old Testament Prophecies Concerning the Kingdom

Just about every Old Testament prophet anticipated the coming kingdom of God on earth. Just consider some of these prophecies:

And He will judge between the nations,
And will render decisions for many peoples;
And they will hammer their swords into plow-
　　shares, and their spears into pruning hooks.
Nation will not lift up sword against nation,
And never again will they learn war. (Isa. 2:4)

"Behold, the days are coming," declares the LORD,
"When I shall raise up for David a righteous Branch;
And He will reign as king and act wisely
And do justice and righteousness in the land.
In His days Judah will be saved,
And Israel will dwell securely;
And this is His name by which He will be called,
'The LORD our righteousness.'" (Jer. 23:5–6)

"But this is the covenant which I will make with the house of Israel after those days," declares the LORD, "I will put My law within them, and on their heart I will write it; and I will be their God, and they shall be My people. And they shall not teach again, each man his neighbor and each man his brother, saying, 'Know the LORD,' for they shall all know Me, from the least of them to the greatest of them," declares the LORD, "for I will forgive their iniquity, and their sin I will remember no more." (Jer. 31:33–34)

"Sing for joy and be glad, O daughter of Zion; for behold I am coming and I will dwell in your midst," declares the LORD. "And many nations will join themselves to the LORD in that day and will become My people. Then I will dwell in your midst, and you will know that the LORD of hosts has sent Me to you. And the LORD will possess Judah as His portion in the holy land, and will again choose Jerusalem." (Zech. 2:10–12)

Some would say that these prophesies were fulfilled when the Jews returned to Palestine (beginning in 538 B.C.) after seventy years of Babylonian captivity. However, there are aspects of these promises that were left unfulfilled. For example, the Israelites did not dwell in the land in safety after their return and were eventually dispersed from the land by the Romans in A.D. 70. Furthermore, one can hardly say that there was any extended spiritual revival in the land when they returned, as Jeremiah anticipated. Everyone did not "know the Lord." Instead, the Israelites quickly fell into apostasy.

Acknowledging these problems, others have wanted to point to heaven as the ultimate fulfillment of these Old Testament prophecies. But there are difficulties with that interpretation as well. Let's look again at one of the best known verses regarding the coming kingdom of God:

> I will also rejoice in Jerusalem, and be glad in My people;
> And there will no longer be heard in her
> The voice of weeping and the sound of crying.
> No longer will there be in it an infant who lives
>   but a few days,
> Or an old man who does not live out his days;
> For the youth will die at the age of one hundred
> And the one who does not reach the age of one hundred
> Shall be thought accursed.
> And they shall build houses and inhabit them;
> They shall also plant vineyards and eat their fruit.
> (Isa. 65:19–21)

As we saw in chapter 1, this verse is obviously not referring to life on the earth as we know it today. When the Jews returned from Babylon to Jerusalem, babies still died and few men lived one hundred years. However, this verse cannot refer to heaven, either, since the Bible clearly says there will be no death in heaven. The Old Testament prophets were not describing the earth as it is or heaven as it will be. Instead, they were anticipating a period in which believers will experience the best of both worlds: heaven on earth!

New Testament Prophecies of the Kingdom

When Christ came to earth the first time, He offered to establish His kingdom on earth. John the Baptist announced, "Repent, for the kingdom of heaven is at hand" (Matt. 4:17). Jesus instructed His disciples to proclaim the coming of His kingdom: "And as you go, preach, saying, 'The kingdom of heaven is at hand'" (Matt. 10:7). Had the Jews received Christ as the Messiah, I believe He would have established His kingdom on earth at that moment.

But what about the Cross? If Christ had been installed as king of the Jews, there would have been no crucifixion. And if there had been no crucifixion, there would be no salvation. Obviously, God knew all along that Israel would reject Christ. And as the apostle Paul explained, God used Israel's rejection to accomplish His ultimate plan. Nevertheless, Christ's offer of a kingdom was legitimate.

But when Israel formally rejected Christ as Messiah (an event recorded in Matt. 12:14–15), Christ's kingdom on earth was not forfeited but simply postponed. The apostles clearly understood this, as evidenced by their question to Jesus before He ascended into heaven:

> "Lord, is it at this time You are restoring the kingdom to Israel?" (Acts 1:6)

Let's pause here and consider that question and some possible answers Jesus could have offered. Suppose for the last several months I have been telling my two little girls, "One day soon I am going to take you to Six Flags over Texas [an area amusement park]." Several days before I leave for an out-of-town speaking engagement my girls ask, "Dad, are you going to take us to Six Flags before you leave?" It would be a natural question. Children are experts at keeping track of promises made, broken, and unfulfilled! Since I am about to depart, they are anxious for me to make good on my promise.

Jesus had promised His disciples something much more important than a trip to an amusement park. He had promised to fulfill the hope of the Old Testament prophets and establish His kingdom on earth. The coming kingdom of Christ was so central in His teaching that the disciples naturally wanted to know when this great event would occur.

Imagine for a moment that the disciples had completely misinterpreted Christ's teachings about the Millennium. Suppose that there was not going to be a literal, physical reign of Christ from Jerusalem; that instead, the rule of Christ had already begun in the hearts of the disciples, as the amillennialists claim. Wouldn't this have been a perfect time for Christ to clear up the misunderstanding? "Boys, you have got this thing all wrong. Israel is never going to have the kingdom restored to her. She forfeited those rights when she rejected Me. The kingdom I am offering is spiritual, not physical."

But Jesus never denied that He would one day establish His kingdom on earth. Instead, He said, "It is not for you to know times or epochs which the Father has fixed by His own authority" (Acts 1:7). The disciples did not misunderstand the nature of the coming kingdom, but simply the timing of it. Christ *would* return to establish His kingdom according to God's timetable, not theirs.

Thus, when we come to the Revelation we finally see the kingdom of Christ established on the earth. Listen to the announcement of the angel when Christ returns to earth:

> And the seventh angel sounded; and there arose loud voices in heaven, saying, "The kingdom of the world has become the kingdom of our Lord, and of His Christ; and He will reign forever and ever." (Rev. 11:15)

This declaration signals the beginning of Christ's physical rule on the earth—a rule prophesied by the prophets, anticipated by the apostles, and fulfilled by Christ.

Four Things Every Christian Should Know about the Millennium

Up to this point we have defined the Millennium, examined differing views of the Millennium, and established the scriptural basis for the Millennium in both the Old and New Testaments. But what is life in the Millennium actually going to be like for those of us who are believers? If all of this discussion about the Millennium has seemed a little academic, allow me to suggest some aspects of this thousand-year period of time that should be of interest to *you*.

1. Only Christians Will Enter into the Millennium

The coming kingdom of Christ is reserved for believers only. Although a number of people will be killed during the

First order of business

Great Tribulation, many others will survive. Some of those survivors will be Christians; others will be unbelievers. When Christ returns to earth, His first order of business will be to preside over a series of judgments described in Matthew 25. Those who survive the judgments will be welcomed into the Millennium; those who don't will be cast into the eternal lake of fire. Look at what Jesus had to say about those judgments:

> But when the Son of Man comes in His glory, and all the angels with Him, then He will sit on His glorious throne. And all the nations will be gathered before Him; and He will separate them from one another, as the shepherd separates the sheep from the goats; and He will put the sheep on His right, and the goats on the left. Then the King will say to those on His right, "Come, you who are blessed of My Father, inherit the kingdom prepared for you from the foundation of the world."
> . . . Then He will also say to those on His left, "Depart from Me, accursed ones, into the eternal fire which has been prepared for the devil and his angels." (Matt. 25:31–34, 41)

Every Christian needs to understand that there are no second chances for salvation once Christ has returned. Only believers will enter into the Millennium.

2. Christians Will Rule with Christ in the Millennium

Although Christ will be ruling the world from David's throne in Jerusalem, He will delegate some of His ruling authority to the twelve apostles (Matt. 19:28), to the Christians martyred during the Tribulation (Rev. 20:4), and to those of us who are Christians (2 Tim. 2:12). As we will see in chapter 9, our ruling responsibilities will be determined by our faithfulness to Christ in this life, as illustrated in the parable of the minas recorded in Luke 19:11–27.

A natural question is, "What (or whom) will we rule over in the Millennium?" Although the Bible is not completely clear about this, Scripture does indicate that we will assist Christ in ruling over cities, over other believers, and even over the angels (1 Cor. 6:2–3; Rev. 22:5)! When the apostle Paul was trying to explain to the Corinthians why they should not sue one another in the pagan court and, instead, rely on wise Christians to settle disputes, he used this rationale:

> Or do you not know that the saints will judge the world? And if the world is judged by you, are you not competent to constitute the smallest law courts? Do you not know that we shall judge angels? How much more, matters of this life? (1 Cor. 6:2–3)

3. Jerusalem Will Be the Center of the Millennial Kingdom

Numerous Old Testament prophecies indicate that Christ will reign on earth from the city of Jerusalem (Isa. 2:2–4; Mic. 4:1; Zech. 2:10–11). However, Jerusalem and all of Palestine will undergo a tremendous topological transformation at the Second Coming of Christ, which will result in greater fertility and productivity (Zech. 14:4; Isa. 30:23–24). This enlarged area will also accommodate the division of land among the twelve tribes of Israel described in Ezekiel 48 and the Millennial Temple detailed in Ezekiel 40–46. The centrality of Jerusalem during the Millennium helps explain why Jerusalem will continue to be a hotbed of conflict and controversy until then.

4. Satan Will Be Temporarily Bound during the Millennium

One reason for the peace, righteousness, prosperity, physical healing, and longevity of life that will characterize the Millennium is that Satan will be imprisoned during these one thousand years. Look at how John described this scene in Revelation 20:

> And I saw an angel coming down from heaven, having the key of the abyss and a great chain in his hand. And he laid hold of the dragon, the serpent of old, who is the devil and Satan, and bound him for a thousand years, and threw him into the abyss, and shut it and sealed it over him, so that he should not deceive the nations any longer, until the thousand years were completed; after these things he must be released for a short time. (Rev. 20:1–3)

Who is it that will be bound for one thousand years? Just so that no one misses it, John was as specific as he could be: "the dragon, the serpent of old, who is the devil and Satan." Since the beginning of recorded history, Satan has been deceiving nations and individuals into thinking they can successfully live apart from their Creator. But for the one thousand years of the Millennium, the deceiver will be bound, and the curse he brought into the world will be *partially* lifted. Although believers who are in their natural bodies during the Millennium will live longer than they do today, they will still die, as evidenced in Isaiah 65:20:

> No longer will there be in it an infant who lives
>   but a few days,
> Or an old man who does not live out his days;
> For the youth will die at the age of one hundred
> And the one who does not reach the age of one hundred
> Shall be thought accursed.

I imagine an alarm bell just sounded in your mind: "Believers who are in their natural bodies? What in the world are you talking about, Robert?" Although only Christians will enter into the Millennium, some will enter in their natural bodies, while others will possess their supernatural bodies. Those believers who survive the Tribulation will enter into the Millennium in their natural bodies, while those of us who return with Christ will be in our supernatural bodies that we received at the Rapture. I will explain and support this belief in the next chapter.

One way to understand what the earth will be like during the Millennium is to think of the words *renovate* and *recreate*. Several years ago our church renovated our facilities. The peeling paint, frayed carpets, and inadequate facilities necessitated the project. Although we made vast improvements to the old facility, our church still has the same exterior, and some of our problems remain. But our long-range planning committee is dreaming of one day re-creating our facilities: building a brand-new sanctuary and creating new educational space that will free us from the limitations of the present facility. Right now we are enjoying a renovated church; one day we will experience a re-created church.

In the same way, Christians during the Millennium will be amazed at the improvement of the renovated earth under Christ's rule. Much of the heartache and suffering that are a part of our everyday existence will vanish. But that renovated earth will be nothing compared to the re-created heaven and earth that we will one day enjoy.

EIGHT

The Great White Throne Judgment

arren Wiersbe tells the story about a frontier town where a horse bolted and ran away with a wagon carrying a small boy. Seeing the child in danger, a young man risked his life to stop the runaway wagon. The rescued boy grew up to be a lawless man and one day found himself standing before a judge, awaiting sentencing for a serious crime. The prisoner recognized the judge as the man who, years before, had saved his life, so he pled for mercy on the basis of that earlier experience. But the words from the judge silenced his plea.

"Young man, on that day I was your savior; today, I am your judge, and I sentence you to be hanged."[1]

Two thousand years ago Jesus Christ came to earth as a Savior. He suffered a humiliating and excruciating death to save us from the consequences of our sin. The next time He comes, however, He will come as a Judge and will say to those who have rejected Him, "I never knew you; DEPART FROM ME, YOU WHO PRACTICE LAWLESSNESS" (Matt. 7:23). In this chapter we are going to examine Christ's coming judgment of unbelievers, an event commonly referred to as the Great White Throne Judgment.

The Two Resurrections

The beginning of Revelation 20 describes the binding of Satan for one thousand years while Christ reigns over a renovated earth. As we saw in the last chapter, only Christians will enter into the Millennium. Some of the Christians who will enter into the Millennium will be those of us who will return with Jesus Christ in our resurrected bodies we receive at the Rapture (see chapter 4). But in Revelation 20:4, John described another group of Christians he saw reigning with Christ: those Christians who were martyred during the Great Tribulation:

> And I saw thrones, and they sat upon them, and judgment was given to them. And I saw the souls of those who had been beheaded because of the testimony of Jesus and because of the word of God, and those who had not worshiped the beast or his image, and had not received the mark upon their forehead and upon their hand; and they came to life and reigned with Christ for a thousand years. The rest of the dead did not come to life until the thousand years were completed. This is the first resurrection. Blessed and holy is the one who has a part in the first resurrection; over these the second death has no power. (Rev. 20:4–6)

128

This term *first resurrection* introduces us to an important key to understanding Bible prophecy: the two resurrections. The word *resurrection* is a translation of the Greek word *anastasis,* which is found more than forty times in the Bible. The word refers to the raising of a fallen body and, thus, is always used to describe a physical resurrection. We have already seen that when a Christian dies, his spirit goes immediately into the presence of Jesus Christ (2 Cor. 5:8) while his body is placed in the grave awaiting resurrection.

Similarly, as we will see in chapter 10, when an unbeliever dies, his spirit goes to a place of torment, while his body is placed in the grave, awaiting a resurrection to eternal judgment. The Bible treats these two resurrections separately: the first resurrection is for Christians and results in eternal life. The second resurrection is reserved for unbelievers and results in eternal death. That is why John says, "Blessed and holy is the one who has a part in the first resurrection; over these the second death has no power" (Rev. 20:6). Let's take a moment and look at this first resurrection in more detail.

The First Resurrection

My wife announced to me that dinner would be late this evening because she was in charge of the car pool to soccer practice. You know how car pools work. The driver stops at different houses, collecting children and finally depositing them on the soccer field. Obviously, not everyone gets into the car at the same time, but they are all part of the car pool and eventually arrive at the same location. I want you to keep that analogy in mind as we discuss the "first resurrection." In fact, think of the first resurrection as a type of heavenly car pool. All Christians will not receive their resurrected bodies simultaneously. Instead, the Bible teaches that there are three stages (or "pickup points") for the first resurrection.

Some Christians will receive their new bodies at the Rapture, some at the beginning of the Millennium, and some after the Millennium. But every Christian's body is ultimately "picked up" and transported to heaven (remember, our *spirits* go to be immediately with the Lord when we die).

The apostle Paul explained this concept of the "first resurrection" in 1 Corinthians 15, the great resurrection chapter of the Bible. This chapter could be subtitled, "Everything You Ever Wanted to Know about the Resurrection but Were Afraid to Ask." Paul spent the first nineteen verses of this chapter using Old Testament prophecies, eyewitness accounts, theology, and logic to defend the truth of Christ's physical resurrection from the grave. While some of the Corinthian believers were willing to concede Christ's resurrection, they could not believe that they would share in that experience. So beginning in verse 20, Paul demonstrated that Christ's resurrection was not some isolated event, but it was the beginning of an extraordinary process: the resurrection of *every* believer:

> But now Christ has been raised from the dead, the
> first fruits of those who are asleep. (1 Cor. 15:20)

The term *first fruits* doesn't mean much to us, but the Israelites understood exactly what Paul had in mind. Before the Israelites would harvest an entire crop, they would bring a sample of that crop to the priests as an offering (Lev. 23:10). That offering was called "first fruits." Obviously, that offering was not the entire harvest; it was only a small, representative portion of what was to come.

Like some of you, I have stood in front of that empty garden tomb in Jerusalem where the single greatest event in human history occurred. In the early morning hours of that first Easter morning, an angel appeared to a startled band of Roman soldiers and rolled the mighty stone away. In an instant, the power of death was forever broken as Jesus Christ "was declared the Son of God with power by the resurrection from the dead" (Rom. 1:4). But as miraculous as that event was, it was only the tip of the iceberg. One day all Christians are going to experience the same kind of resurrection.

> For as in Adam all die, so also in Christ all shall be made alive. But each in his own order. (1 Cor. 15:22–23)

Every Christian is going to receive a brand-new body (bodies that we will discuss further in chapter 10), but everyone must wait his turn! The key word here is *order*, which comes from the Greek word *tagma*. The word *tagma* is a military term that refers to rank or order. Paul was describing a military parade passing by, with each corps falling into position at the proper time (for those who can't identify with the military, think of the car pool). The first resurrection is like a parade that began when Christ arose from the dead.[2] Throughout history, different Christians fall into their place in the parade at their appointed times. Notice that in this passage, Paul mentions three "pickup points" or places where the corps falls into place:

For as in Adam all die, so also in Christ all shall be made alive. But each in his own order: Christ the first fruits, after that those who are Christ's at His coming, then comes the end, when He delivers up the kingdom to the God and Father, when He has abolished all rule and all authority and power. (1 Cor. 15:22–24)

Perhaps this chart will help you understand the stages of the first resurrection and contrast it with the second resurrection.

1a. "Christ the first fruits." Jesus Christ is the undisputed Leader of this resurrection parade. In Ephesians 4:8, Paul again used this word picture: "When HE ASCENDED ON HIGH, HE LED CAPTIVE A HOST OF CAPTIVES, AND HE GAVE GIFTS TO MEN."

1b and 1c. "After that, those who are Christ's at His coming." As we saw in chapter 4, the term *coming* refers to two events: the Rapture and the Second Coming. Paul probably had both events in mind here. First Thessalonians 4:13–18 and 1 Corinthians 15:51–53 explain that at the Rapture, Christians who have died, as well as those believers alive at the time, will receive their new bodies. But what about those believers who are killed during the Tribulation, as well as the Old Testament saints? They will receive their resurrection bodies at the Second Coming of Christ (seven years after the Rapture). Revelation 20:4 and Daniel 12:1–2 explain this truth.

1d. "Then comes the end, when He delivers up the kingdom." The fourth stage of the first resurrection will occur at the end of the Millennium when those Christians who survived the Tribulation and entered the Millennium in their natural bodies, as well as those born during the Millennium and choose to follow Christ, will receive their new bodies. (I will explain this further in the next section).

The Second Resurrection *unbelievers*

2. "And the sea gave up the dead which were in it, and death and Hades gave up the dead which were in them" (Rev. 20:13). Unlike the first resurrection, the second resurrection is a single event that will include all of the unsaved dead since the time of Adam.

The purpose of the first resurrection is that believers might receive their promised inheritance of a new body. Our new bodies will be identical to the resurrected body of Christ (see 1 John 3:2) and, therefore, will be free from sin, suffering, and death.

The purpose of the second resurrection is for unbelievers to receive the punishment due them for their rejection of Christ. It is that final judgment of unbelievers that the apostle John described in the last half of Revelation 20. But before that final judgment can occur, there is one last event that must transpire.

133

The Unleashing of Satan

Last night I was awakened by the chirping of a cricket. As I stealthily tiptoed into our bathroom, I noticed some movement in the planter box around the bathtub (we grow big crickets in Texas). Realizing that I had located the enemy, I jumped into the bathtub, pulled back the silk plants, and saw the creature running for its life. I quickly scooped him into my hand and started to deposit him in the watery grave of our toilet, when I was suddenly struck by compassion and let him go.

Do you believe that happened? Not on your life. When I finally captured that annoying insect, I wasn't about to release him. He had caused me too much trouble ever to merit a second chance . . . which is why I find Revelation 20:7 a little difficult to understand.

Remember that at the beginning of the Millennium the angel will lay hold of Satan and deposit him into the abyss. For the next one thousand years, the whole earth will enjoy a rest from most of the sin and suffering caused by the evil one. But then notice what will happen:

> And when the thousand years are completed, Satan will be released from his prison, and will come out to deceive the nations which are in the four corners of the earth, Gog and Magog, to gather them together for the war; the number of them is like the sand of the seashore. And they came up on the broad plain of the earth and surrounded the camp of the saints and the beloved city, and fire came down from heaven and devoured them. (Rev. 20:7–9)

At the end of the Millennium, God will unleash Satan from the abyss and give him one last opportunity to deceive the world. John said in Revelation that in spite of the fact that Christ will have ruled the earth for a thousand years with perfect righteousness, a multitude of people will choose to follow Satan and, as a result, will suffer God's judgment.

For any thinking person, this raises a number of disturbing questions.

- Who are these people who choose to follow Satan in his final rebellion?

- Is it possible that genuine Christians could be deceived at the last moment and spend eternity in hell?

- Why does Revelation 20:3 say that God *must* release Satan "for a short time?"

First things first. Let's establish that it is impossible for a Christian ever to lose his salvation. Jesus said in John 10:28, "And I give eternal life to them, and they shall never perish; and no one shall snatch them out of My hand." Paul declared in Romans 11:29, "For the gifts and the calling of God are irrevocable." Whoever these people are who choose to follow Satan at the end of the Millennium, they are not believers.

"But Robert, you said that only Christians will enter the Millennium. So how could these people who choose to follow Satan at the end of the Millennium be anyone other than Christians?" This is where an understanding of the different stages of the first resurrection helps us.

Remember that not every Christian will receive his new body at the same time. When Christ returns at the Second

Coming to establish His millennial kingdom, He will return with those of us who received our new bodies at the Rapture. There will be another group of people saved and martyred during the Tribulation who will receive their new bodies at the Second Coming, prior to the Millennium. But there is a final group of Christians who will enter the Millennium in their natural bodies (see 1d on the chart). These are the people who will be saved during the Tribulation but not martyred. This means that during the Millennium there will be Christians who are in their resurrected bodies along with Christians who are in their natural bodies.

I'll admit that this seems a little bizarre, but such an arrangement answers a number of questions about the Millennium. For example, how is it that people will be born and will die in the Millennium as prophesied in Isaiah 65:20?

> No longer will there be in it an infant who lives
> but a few days,
> Or an old man who does not live out his days;
> For the youth will die at the age of one hundred
> And the one who does not reach the age of one hundred
> Shall be thought accursed.

We know from Jesus' teaching in Luke 20:35–36 that Christians will not be able to procreate in their resurrected bodies. Furthermore, we know that our new bodies will never die (Rev. 21:4). Finally, we know that only Christians enter into the Millennium. Thus, the only explanation for birth and death in the Millennium is that some Christians will enter in to this thousand-year period of time in their natural bodies. It is these Christians who will produce children and eventually die (whether they receive their new bodies instantly or wait until the end of the Millennium is unclear).

Such an explanation also answers the questions related to Satan's final rebellion at the conclusion of the Millennium. I believe that those who choose to follow Satan will be some of the children born during the millennial reign of Christ. Although these children will be the offspring of genuine believers, they will have to make an individual choice to follow Christ. Such a choice is only possible if God releases Satan and provides them with an alternative. Amazingly, some of these who have enjoyed the millennial blessings of Christ will nevertheless choose to follow Satan. Their rebellion should lay to rest forever the myth that environment determines behavior. Except for Eden, the Millennium will be the best environment mankind has ever experienced. Nevertheless, the sin nature that exists in every human heart will cause some to rebel against Christ.

So after every person in every age has been given an opportunity to trust in Christ, God will be ready for the final judgment of mankind.

The Great White Throne Judgment

Contrary to what some people believe, there is not one final judgment that includes believers and unbelievers. Instead, non-Christians are judged separately from Christians at a judgment commonly referred to as the Great White Throne Judgment, described in Revelation 20:11–15.

The Description of the White Throne Judgment

> And I saw a great white throne and Him who sat
> upon it, from whose presence earth and heaven
> fled away, and no place was found for them. (Rev.
> 20:11)

After Satan's final rebellion, God will cast him into the
lake of fire for an eternity of punishment (see Rev. 20:10).
Apparently God then will destroy the present heaven and earth
in preparation for the new heaven and earth. Prior to the Great
Tribulation, Revelation 4:2–5 pictures God sitting on a throne
surrounded by a rainbow, flashes of lightning, and other believers. But Revelation 20:11 describes a solitary throne suspended
in space. This is obviously a different throne with a different
Occupant. Jesus Christ is seated on this throne as He prepares
to judge those who have rejected Him.

The Subjects of the Great White Throne Judgment

> And I saw the dead, the great and the small, stand-
> ing before the throne, . . . And the sea gave up the
> dead which were in it, and death and Hades gave
> up the dead which were in them; and they were
> judged, every one of them according to their
> deeds. (Rev. 20:12–13)

Some fine Bible students want to simplify matters by
insisting that there is only one final judgment for both believers
and unbelievers. When Christ returns to earth, believers and
unbelievers will stand before Christ to be commended or

138

condemned. Those who are commended will be welcomed into heaven; those who are condemned will be dispatched to hell, some believe. But a careful study of the word translated "Hades" reveals that since the ascension of Christ this word has been used to describe the abiding place of the unsaved dead (we will distinguish between "Hades" and "hell" in chapter 10). Thus, the only people involved in the Great White Throne Judgment are the unsaved dead who are presently occupying Hades.

The Basis for the White Throne Judgment

By what standard will Christ judge the unbelievers who stand before Him at the White Throne Judgment? It may surprise you to learn that unbelievers will be judged by their *works*. Read carefully Revelation 20:12–13:

> And I saw the dead, the great and the small, standing before the throne, and the books were opened; and another book was opened, which is the book of life; and the dead were judged from the things which were written in the books, *according to their deeds*. And the sea gave up the dead which were in it, and death and Hades gave up the dead which were in them; and they were judged, every one of them *according to their deeds*. (Author emphasis)

God keeps two sets of books on each of us. First, there is "the book of life" which contains the name of every believer who has trusted in Christ. Revelation 13:8 and Revelation 17:8 explain that the name of every believer was entered into this book before the foundation of the world. Is that because God *knew* beforehand who would trust in Christ or because He *determined* beforehand who would trust in Christ? Sorry, but we will have to save those questions for another book. The point here is that those whose names are written in this book of life will have nothing to fear, but those whose names do not appear in the book of life will have *everything* to fear.

> And if anyone's name was not found written in the book of life, he was thrown into the lake of fire. (Rev. 20:15)

But God also keeps a second set of books that record all of our deeds: the good, the bad, and the ugly. Every word, every thought, every action is carefully noted in our permanent record:

- The money you gave to United Way last year.

- The time you spent volunteering at hospice while in college.

- The lustful thought you had about your neighbor last week.

- The hateful words you said to your mate ten years ago.

- The income you failed to report on your 1986 tax return.

No good deed goes unnoted, and no sin goes unrecorded. It is all in "the books." Since God will not find the names of unbelievers written in the book of life, He will open this second set of books to judge unbelievers according to their works.

One of the saddest aspects to me about this whole judgment is the confidence many unbelievers will feel when this judgment begins. After the initial shock of standing before the Lord Jesus Christ, some unbelievers will breathe a sigh of relief when the Lord announces that they will be judged by their works. "By our works? This will be easy. I may not be perfect, but I'm no Adolf Hitler, either. I've loved my family, paid my taxes, and lived by the Golden Rule. Now, when do I get to check out those streets of gold I've heard about?" Ironically, it will be their misplaced confidence in their own righteousness that will land them before the Great White Throne.

The non-Christian's optimism suddenly will turn to despair, however, when he realizes that the standard by which his life is judged is not his neighbor, but Jesus Christ Himself. One of the greatest misconceptions among non-Christians is that God grades on the curve. As long as we meet some minimum standards of decency, we can expect to be welcomed into heaven, they maintain. But Acts 17:31 tells us that the standard by which we will be judged will be the perfect life of Jesus Christ:

> Because He has fixed a day in which He will judge
> the world in righteousness through a Man whom
> He has appointed, having furnished proof to all
> men by raising Him from the dead.

At the Great White Throne Judgment, every unbeliever will realize how far short he has fallen from the perfect righteousness of Jesus Christ.

The Result of the White Throne Judgment

What is the fate of those who are judged at the Great White Throne? Everyone who is resurrected for that judgment will be cast into to the lake of fire:

> And death and Hades were thrown into the lake of fire. This is the second death, the lake of fire. And if anyone's name was not found written in the book of life, he was thrown into the lake of fire. (Rev. 20:14–15)

We are going to study this lake of fire in more detail in chapter 10. But notice that the lake of fire is a place of eternal suffering. We saw in Revelation 20:10 that Satan, the beast, and the false prophet were cast into this horrible place of punishment where they were "tormented day and night forever and ever." Imagine the worst pain you have ever experienced. As excruciating as that pain was, at least there was some relief that eventually came. But imagine experiencing that pain without any relief for millions, billions, and trillions of years. That is the horror that awaits those who will be judged at the Great White Throne.

People frequently ask me, "How could a loving God ever sentence anyone to that kind of punishment?" The simple answer is that people *choose* to go to hell. Those participants in the Great White Throne Judgment have said, in effect, "I do not need Jesus Christ as my Savior. If God is going to judge me, I'll take my chances and let Him judge me by my works." Thus, God will grant them their wish and judge them by their deeds.

The only way a holy God can allow any of us to enter heaven is by insisting that our righteousness equal that of His Son Jesus Christ. "That's impossible," you say. "I could never be as good as Jesus was." That's the point! When I trust in Christ as my Savior, God takes the righteousness of His Son and wraps it around me. His righteousness becomes my righteousness.

Perhaps this illustration will help. Imagine a book called *The Life and Times of Jesus Christ*. This book contains all the words, thoughts, and deeds of the only perfect Man who has ever lived. Now imagine another book titled *The Life and Times of [Your Name]*. This book is a record of everything you have ever done, said, or thought. Such a book reads like a supermarket tabloid. Now imagine God stripping both books of their covers. Then He takes the cover of the book about Jesus' life, and he wraps it around the book of your life story. Next, God takes the cover of your book and wraps it around *The Life and Times of Jesus Christ*. When God opens the book about Jesus Christ, He reads a book about your lies, corruption, and immorality. Jesus gets the blame for your sin. But when God opens the book about you, He reads a story about the perfection, purity, and complete obedience of His own Son. You get the credit for Jesus' perfect life.[3]

That is what the doctrine of justification is all about. God takes your sin and credits it to Jesus, and He takes Jesus' righteousness and credits it to your account. Paul explained it this way:

He made Him who knew no sin to be sin on our behalf, that we might become the righteousness of God in Him. (2 Cor. 5:21)

As we close this chapter, let me ask you the most important question of all: what are you depending on to get you into
heaven? Good deeds? Baptism? Church membership? A religious relative? Only those who understand their sinfulness and
wrap themselves in the righteousness of Jesus Christ will escape
the Great White Throne Judgment. If you would like to receive
the forgiveness that Christ offers you, may I suggest you pray
this prayer:

Dear God,
I realize that I have fallen short of Your standards. I know
that I have sinned in many ways and deserve to be punished by
You. But I believe with all of my heart that You sent Jesus Christ
to die for me. I believe that when Jesus hung on that cross, He
took the punishment that I deserve. And now I am trusting in
Him alone to save me from my sins.
Thank You for forgiving me, and help me to live for You.
In Jesus' name,
Amen.

If you prayed that prayer sincerely, you can know that
not only will you escape the horror of hell, but you can also
look forward to an event we will discuss in the next chapter.

Rewards in Heaven

My friend Howard Hendricks tells the story about a downhill slalom racer who was greeted at the bottom of the course by his ski coach. "The good news is that you arrived at the finish marker faster than any of my other students. In fact, your time was the fastest ever on this course, perhaps even faster than the world record." But the coach wasn't finished. "The bad news is that you missed nearly every flag and are disqualified." To which the novice skier replied, "Flags? What flags?"

An expert skier understands that the route he takes to get downhill is just as critical as reaching the goal. A good basketball player realizes that even more important than making a basket is making sure he is aiming toward the *right* basket.

Unfortunately, many Christians fail to understand a similar truth. Making it to heaven should not be the only goal of a believer.

The Bible teaches that while all Christians will cross the "finish line," some will experience the loss of eternal rewards because their works have been disqualified by the Judge.[1] The result of such a loss will be severe disappointment and lasting regret.

"Wait a minute," you protest. "Are you trying to tell me that it is possible I could be disappointed in heaven?" Absolutely. One of the greatest myths about eternity is that all Christians will experience the same kind of heaven and all unbelievers will experience the same kind of hell. Such a belief is illogical, and more importantly, unbiblical. In this chapter we are going to examine the reality of rewards in heaven.

Future Judgments

In the last chapter we discussed the judgment of all unbelievers known as the Great White Throne Judgment. Occurring at the end of the Millennium, this judgment will be reserved for those who have refused to trust in Christ as Savior. Because they have rejected God's grace, they will be judged by their works. The result of the judgment will be that every unbeliever will be cast into the lake of fire. Why? Because the unbeliever's deeds, as good as they may be, will fail to measure up to the perfection required by God.

Although the Great White Throne Judgment is the *final* judgment of unbelievers, it is not the only judgment of unbelievers. Matthew 25:31–46 teaches that when Christ returns to earth prior to the beginning of His millennial kingdom, He will judge the survivors of the Tribulation period. Although a large portion of the world's population will be destroyed during the

Tribulation, many will escape death. Since only believers will be welcomed into the Millennium, it will be necessary for Christ to deal with the surviving unbelievers. While some Bible scholars see a whole series of judgments occurring at the Second Coming of Christ (a judgment of nations, a judgment of Jewish Tribulation survivors, a judgment of Gentile Tribulation survivors, a judgment of martyred Tribulation saints and so on), I think it makes more sense to see one judgment:

> "But when the Son of Man comes in His glory, and all the angels with Him, then He will sit on His glorious throne. And all the nations will be gathered before Him; and He will separate them from one another, as the shepherd separates the sheep from the goats; and He will put the sheep on His right, and the goats on the left. Then the King will say to those on His right, 'Come, you who are blessed of My Father, inherit the kingdom prepared for you from the foundation of the world. For I was hungry, and you gave Me something to eat; I was thirsty, and you gave Me drink; I was a stranger, and you invited Me in. . . . Truly I say to you, to the extent that you did it to one of these brothers of Mine, even the least of them, you did it to Me.' Then He will also say to those on His left, 'Depart from Me, accursed ones, into the eternal fire which has been prepared for the devil and his angels.'" (Matt. 25:31–35, 40–41)

As we saw in chapter 1, these verses are some of the most misunderstood and misapplied passages of Scripture. Contrary to popular opinion, this is not a general command to clothe, feed, and care for the neglected. Instead, it is an explanation of a specific judgment for a specific group of people (Tribulation survivors) that will occur when Christ returns to earth. Those who have given aid to the 144,000 Jewish witnesses (see chapter 5) will have demonstrated their faith in the gospel message and will be ushered into Christ's kingdom. Those who reject the ministry of the 144,000 will be cast into the lake of fire—the same lake of fire that will serve as the eternal destination of other unbelievers.

But what about the rest of us who are not a part of this judgment or the Great White Throne Judgment?

- Should we be concerned about God's evaluation of our lives?

- Is there a time when we will have to account for our words, actions, thoughts, and motivations?

- Does how we live our life now make any difference in the kind of eternity we will experience?

The answer to all of the above questions is "yes." One day every Christian will stand before Christ at an event referred to in Scripture as "the judgment seat of Christ."

The Reality of the Judgment Seat of Christ

Last year we took a group of church members to visit the ancient city of Corinth where the apostle Paul ministered for eighteen months. Acts 18 tells us that many "were believing and being baptized" in Corinth because of Paul's ministry (Acts 18:8). But many were also agitated by Paul's preaching, so they hauled him before the Roman proconsul Gallio to give an account for his actions:

> But while Gallio was proconsul of Achaia, the Jews with one accord rose up against Paul and brought him before the judgment seat. (Acts 18:12)

The word translated "judgment seat" is the Greek word *bema*. It refers to a raised platform on which a ruler or judge would sit to pronounce his decree. We actually stood on the spot where the apostle Paul faced Gallio as the Roman ruler sat on the "judgment seat." I imagined what it must have been like to stand, shackled in chains, before an indifferent ruler who with a single word could extinguish my life. But Paul never backed down. What was the source of his unyielding courage? It was the realization that one day he would stand before another "judgment seat" and give an account of his life to the true Judge of the universe, the Lord Jesus Christ. Paul later used this imagery of the "judgment seat" in reminding the Corinthians of a coming evaluation of each of our lives:

> Therefore also we have as our ambition, whether at home or absent, to be pleasing to Him. For we must all appear before the judgment seat of Christ, that each one may be recompensed for his deeds in the body, according to what he has done, whether good or bad. (2 Cor. 5:9–10)

You will notice that Paul said, "*we* must all appear," not "*they* must all appear." Paul was obviously including himself in this judgment that will be reserved for Christians. Every Christian will one day answer to Christ for every thought, word, action, and motivation of his earthly life. But unlike the Great White Throne Judgment, the purpose of this judgment is not condemnation, but evaluation.

Every year I try to have a complete physical. For several hours I am poked, pinched, and prodded in just about every part of my anatomy. But for me the worst part of the test is being submerged in what is affectionately known as "the fat tank." The doctor has me remove all of my clothing and climb into a basket suspended above a pool of water. Then I am lowered into the water, holding my breath for a seemingly interminable amount of time while the doctor determines my percentage of body fat. If that is not bad enough, I then am forced to stand completely naked in front of the doctor while he uses some kind of torture device to grab different parts of my body and calculate my body fat by a different method. Every chocolate chip cookie I have ever eaten, every morning I have rolled over in bed and said, "No exercise today," every late night trip to the refrigerator is suddenly on display to my physician.

At the end of the ordeal, the doctor has a conference with me in his office. After a few pleasantries, he opens the folder containing the results of my exam. First, he commends me for the good things I have done: my exercise program, the results of the treadmill tests, the bowl of Bran Flakes I consume every morning. But then his smile turns to a frown. "Now, let's talk about your body fat. We need to shave a few percentage points off that. And your cholesterol needs to be lowered. You need to cut back on all of that coffee." The doctor commends me for the good things I have done and chides me for my deficiencies.

Similarly, at the judgment seat of Christ (which probably will occur immediately after the Rapture) every aspect of our lives will be evaluated by Christ. Yet, many Christians have difficulty accepting that truth.

- "Doesn't becoming a Christian mean that all of my sins have been forgiven?"

- "I thought that when God forgave my mistakes He forgot them."

- "Aren't my good works worthless before God?"

We will answer those questions in a moment. But first, let's establish the fact that Christians are indeed going to have their works—all of them—judged by Christ. First Corinthians 3:10–15 is the most detailed passage in the New Testament concerning the judgment seat of Christ. Notice what Paul says about the completeness of this judgment:

> *Each* man's work will become evident; for the day will show it, because it is to be revealed with fire; and the fire itself will test the quality of each man's work. (1 Cor. 3:13, Author emphasis)

Consider again Paul's words in 2 Corinthians 5:10:

> For we must all appear before the judgment seat of Christ, that each one may be recompensed for his deeds in the body, according to what he has done, *whether good or bad.* (Author emphasis)

Both of these passages describe the completeness of this judgment. The *bema* judgment is for *every* Christian and will cover *all* of our works. I read somewhere that there is a central location on the Worldwide Web that records all of the "hits" by various subscribers. Think about it. There is someone who has a record of every website you have ever contacted. Similarly, God has a record of our every word, thought, action, and motivation, and one day He will bring them all to light. Some Christians reject this truth because they have been taught that neither their sins nor their good deeds make any difference to God once they became a Christian.

The judgment seat of Christ in no way invalidates the forgiveness we have received from Christ. As we saw in the last chapter, when we trust in Jesus Christ as our Savior, we are wrapping ourselves in the righteousness of Christ. (Remember the illustrations of the two books?) God no longer sees our sin, but He sees the perfection of His own Son. Nevertheless, the fact that we have been declared "not guilty" before God and are guaranteed a place in heaven does not negate the possibility of God's judgment of our works. For example, consider King David in the Old Testament and Ananias and Sapphira in the New Testament. They were all believers who had been forgiven of their sins and are in heaven today. Yet their sins still carried serious consequences. Their salvation did not exempt them from God's evaluation.

For those who want to discount the importance of our works, we need to draw an important distinction. Although our works are worthless to secure our *place* in heaven, they will play a large role in determining our *rank* in heaven. The apostle Paul draws a distinction between works before salvation and works after salvation:

For by grace you have been saved through faith;
and that not of yourselves, it is the gift of God; not
as a result of works, that no one should boast. For
we are His workmanship, created in Christ Jesus
for good works, which God prepared beforehand,
that we should walk in them. (Eph. 2:8–10)

Before we are saved, our works are only sufficient to condemn us. But once we become a Christian, our works are of
great importance to God. In the last section of this chapter, we
will discuss the specific relationship between works and
rewards.

The Basis for the Judgment Seat of Christ

By what standard will our works be evaluated at the
judgment seat of Christ? Paul answered that question clearly in
1 Corinthians 3:

For no man can lay a foundation other than the
one which is laid, which is Jesus Christ. Now if
any man builds upon the foundation with gold,
silver, precious stones, wood, hay, straw, each
man's work will become evident; for the day will
show it, because it is to be revealed with fire; and
the fire itself will test the quality of each man's
work. (1 Cor. 3:11–13)

Imagine that your father, a multibillionaire, purchases
two one-acre tracts of land for you and a sibling. He pours a
foundation on each piece of land and then gives each of you one

million dollars, with these instructions: "I am going to give you one year to build the most beautiful home you can construct. At the end of the year, the one who builds the most elaborate house will receive twice as much of my estate as the other." You and your sibling are thrilled with the possibility.

You begin work immediately. You hire architects to draw up the plans, you ask contractors for estimates, and you establish a rigid schedule to make sure you complete your work on time. When the deadline arrives, you have a home that rivals the Taj Mahal.

However, your sibling is not as industrious. Family responsibilities, work, and hobbies keep him from the task at hand. Not only that, but he has some immediate needs for that one million dollars: college tuition, a new car, and a swimming pool. The night before the deadline, he decides to get busy and construct the best home he can with little money and only a few hours of time. A grass hut is all he can manage to build.

The next morning, your father surveys the two homes. He praises you for your efforts and rewards you with the promise of a large portion of his vast estate. As he walks around your sibling's grass hut, however, he expresses his disappointment. As a result of procrastination and squandering of resources, your sibling forfeited billions of dollars of future wealth. He is still in the family, but he does not receive the same reward.

Paul said that when we become a Christian, we all have the same foundation for our lives: Jesus Christ. Nevertheless, we choose the kind of life we want to construct upon that foundation. Some choose to build palaces that will receive our Father's commendation; others squander their time and resources and build grass huts that receive our Father's condemnation. The apostle Paul explained two specific criteria by which our lives will be judged.

The Durability of Our Life

We can build our lives with "gold, silver, precious stones" or with "wood, hay, and straw." Obviously the former represents those things which are valuable and lasting; the latter category represents those things which are cheap and temporal. Let's get specific. A life that is built around the pursuit of a career, or financial gain, or sensual delights is a life built with wood, hay, and straw. Such a life will not survive the fire of God's judgment. However, a life that is built around serving Christ, modeling His character, and building His kingdom is one that will stand the test of time.

What is the focus of your life? Having trouble answering that question? Then I invite you to honestly answer these questions:

- What do I think about most often?

- What do I talk about most often?

- If someone were to give me $25,000, how would I spend it?

Your answer to those questions will quickly reveal your life's focus. Are you building a life with gold, silver, and precious stones or with wood, hay, and straw?

The Motives of Our Life

Sometimes *why* we do something can be just as important as *what* we do. At the judgment seat of Christ, God will examine the "whys" as well as the "whats" of our lives:

> Therefore do not go on passing judgment before
> the time, but wait until the Lord comes who will
> both bring to light the things hidden in the dark-
> ness and disclose the motives of men's hearts; and
> then each man's praise will come to him from
> God. (1 Cor. 4:5)

If I share the gospel with a person out of a genuine concern for him, God counts that as "gold." However, if my motive is to exalt myself as a "soul-winner" to other Christians, that is labeled as "wood." If I give my money to God as an act of worship and obedience, God views that as silver. But if my motivation is recognition by others, my actions are deemed "straw." Proverbs 16:2 reminds us that "all the ways of a man are clean in his own sight, But the LORD weighs the motives."

One word of caution. Don't use this truth as a cop-out for obedience. Some people rationalize their lack of faithfulness to Christ by saying, "If my heart is not in giving, witnessing, or service, then what is the point in doing it?" One of the purest motivations for obeying Christ is faith—faith that God is going to reward me for serving Him, even when my heart is not in it. Even though I really don't want to give my money to the church this month, I do so, believing that God will one day reward my obedience. Although I may not feel like witnessing to my friend, I do so, believing that one day God will honor my efforts. Even though I would rather be at the lake on Sunday, I teach my first-grade Sunday school class believing that there will be future compensation for my obedience.

"Serving God for rewards is a wrong motivation" you say? Consider Abraham's motivation for obeying God and leaving his home in Ur. "For he was looking for the city which has foundations, whose architect and builder is God" (Heb. 11:10). Or think about Moses who chose "to endure ill-treatment with the people of God, than to enjoy the passing pleasures of sin; considering the reproach of Christ greater riches than the treasures of Egypt; for he was looking to the *reward*" (Heb. 11:25–26, Author emphasis). The promise of a future reward was Abraham's and Moses' motivation for obedience.

The Results of the Judgment Seat of Christ

If I just make it into heaven, won't that be reward enough? Will the results of God's evaluation of our lives make any real difference in eternity? Paul didn't hesitate in answering those questions. There are real and measurable consequences we will experience at the judgment seat of Christ:

> If any man's work which he has built upon it remains, he shall receive a reward. If any man's work is burned up, he shall suffer loss; but he himself shall be saved, yet so as through fire. (1 Cor. 3:14–15)

Rewards in Heaven

Those whose actions and motivations are judged as "silver, gold, and precious stones" will receive rewards. The Bible speaks of "crowns" that Christians will receive in heaven, including the "crown of glory" (1 Pet. 5:4) for those who serve in leadership in a church; the "crown of exultation" (1 Thess. 2:19–20), which is associated with evangelism; the "crown of life" (James 1:12; Rev. 2:10), which is reserved for those who endure the trials of life; and "the crown of righteousness," which is bestowed on those who live obediently in anticipation of the Lord's return (2 Tim. 4:6–8). Some believe that these are actual crowns we will wear in heaven; however, others like myself see these crowns as symbolic of very real benefits given to those who succeed at the judgment seat of Christ. Those benefits include privileges, praise, and position.

Privileges. Several years ago we took our family to Disney World. If you have ever been, you know that for a single price you can enter the park and enjoy all of the attractions. However, those who are willing to pay more can have some additional benefits: early entrance into the park, nicer accommodations, a chance to eat breakfast with Mickey and Minnie (don't miss that one).

In the same way, the Bible teaches that some Christians will enjoy special benefits in heaven, including a special entrance into the kingdom of God (2 Pet. 1:11), special access to the tree of life (Rev. 2:7), and even special treatment by Christ Himself (Luke 12:37).[2] I don't pretend to understand what all of these benefits mean, but they are nevertheless real and worth attaining.

Praise. Can you recall a time when your parent said to you, "I'm so proud of you. You are a wonderful daughter [or son]"? Has your employer ever pulled you aside and said, "You're doing a great job. I appreciate all you do for this organization"? Such affirmations can keep you going for weeks! Now, imagine hearing the Creator of the universe say to you, "Well done, good and faithful servant." That is a reward that will be reserved for obedient Christians (Matt. 25:21).

Positions. If you think praise is cheap, then consider the benefits that will accompany those words of praise from the Master:

> "Well done, good and faithful slave; you were faithful with a few things, I will put you in charge of many things, enter into the joy of your master." (Matt. 25:21)

Jesus was teaching that our faithfulness in this life will determine what responsibility we will have in the new heaven and earth. Paul taught the same truth in 2 Timothy 2:12: "If we endure, we shall also reign with Him." One day we will be corulers with Christ over the angels, the planets, and the nations. Most of us fail to grasp the vastness of God's creation. The Hubble telescope recently relayed from space images of galaxies that are 12 billion times 6 trillion miles away.[3] God will delegate to us responsibility for governing those 50 billion galaxies, based on our trustworthiness in this life.

I know what you are thinking. "I'm tired. The last thing I want in heaven is *more* responsibility. I just want to float on a cloud somewhere. That will be enough for me." Yet, the Book of Genesis tells us that we were designed in God's image to work and rule, just as Adam and Eve did. God meant for us to be invigorated, not debilitated, by labor. Only after sin entered the world did work become tedious and difficult. But in the new creation, all the hindrances to enjoying work will be removed: tired bodies, inadequate compensation, burdensome regulations, and soured relationships. We will enjoy the responsibility God gives us, but the degree of fulfillment we experience will depend upon our faithfulness to Christ in this life.

Whatever these crowns represent, the Word of God teaches that they represent rewards that are definitely worth pursuing.

Loss

Unfortunately, the judgment seat of Christ will also result in a loss of rewards for other Christians:

> If any man's work is burned up, he shall suffer loss; but he himself shall be saved, yet so as through fire. (1 Cor. 3:15)

Don't allow anyone to mislead you. Heaven will not be the same for everyone. Those who have built their lives around trivial pursuits will experience real, measurable loss in heaven. Although their salvation is secure ("he himself shall be saved"), they will endure real and lasting regret as they see what could have been theirs had they spent their life pursing the eternal, instead of the temporal.

When I have taught on this subject before, some people have objected saying, "What you are describing sounds like hell instead of heaven. If heaven is a place of joy, how is it that some Christians will also experience regret over the loss of rewards?"

Perhaps this analogy will help you understand how heaven will be a place of both joy and regret for some Christians. Last year my insurance agent said, "Robert, I've been reviewing your homeowner's policy, and I believe you are underinsured by fifty thousand dollars. I would recommend that you increase your coverage." We heeded his advice and increased our coverage. But suppose I had said, "Let me think about it, and I'll get back to you in a few weeks." That very night Amy and I are awakened by the smell of smoke. Hearing the screams of our two girls, we stumble through the thick fog until we reach their bedrooms. Grabbing our daughters, we grope through the darkness, searching for a way out. But all of the exits are blocked, so we throw a chair through the window and climb through the broken glass. Once safely outside, we watch in horror as our home is consumed by the flames.

What emotions do I feel at that moment? Certainly I am relieved that my family made it through the fire. No one could place a price tag on their lives. Nevertheless, I also feel a deep sense of regret as I consider the financial loss I am about to experience because I made a wrong choice about my insurance. My joy of survival is tempered by my feelings of regret.[4]

The apostle Paul was saying that many Christians will one day feel overwhelming gratitude for escaping the flames of hell. But that gratitude will be mixed with a sense of loss as they realize what might have been theirs had they lived more faithfully for Christ.

Erwin Lutzer told the story of a beggar in India who saw a wealthy rajah come toward him, riding in his beautiful chariot. The beggar stood by the side of the road, holding out his bowl of rice, hoping for a handout. To his surprise, the rajah stopped and demanded, "Give me some of your rice!" The beggar was angry at the thought of such a wealthy man demanding some of his scarce supply of rice. He begrudgingly gave the rajah one grain of rice. "I want more." So the beggar gave him another grain. "More rice, please," the rajah asked. By now, the beggar was seething with resentment, but he handed him one more grain of rice.

After the rajah departed, the beggar looked into the bowl of rice and noticed something glittering. It was a grain of gold, the size of a grain of rice. He looked more carefully and found two more grains of gold. For every grain of rice, a grain of gold.

Lutzer then makes this application. "If we clutch our bowl of rice, we shall lose our reward. If we are faithful and give God each grain, He gives us gold in return. And the gold God gives will survive the fire."[5]

It is the promise of that future reward that caused the apostle Paul to write,

> Therefore also we have as our ambition, whether at home or absent, to be pleasing to Him. For we must all appear before the judgment seat of Christ, that each one may be recompensed for his deeds in the body, according to what he has done, whether good or bad. (2 Cor. 5:9–10)

The Truth about Eternity

I love the story Harold Kushner tells about a man who died after living a godless, immoral life. To his surprise, however, the newly departed found himself in a world of bright sunlight, soft music, and people all dressed in white. "I sure never expected to end up here," he mused to himself. "I suppose God must have a soft spot in His heart for people like me." He turned to one of the figures in white and said, "Can I buy you a drink? I've got something to celebrate." The figure replied, "If you are referring to an alcoholic beverage, we don't serve those here."

"No booze, huh? Well, how about a game of poker? Poker, Black Jack, you name it, we'll play."

"Sorry," the figure dressed in white said, "we don't gamble here either."

The man was mystified. "Then what do you do all day around here?"

"Well, we read the psalms a lot. There is a Bible study every morning and a prayer meeting every afternoon."

"Psalms? Bible study? Prayer meetings? Heaven isn't what it's cracked up to be."

At this point the figure in white smiled and said, "I see that you don't understand. We're in heaven; you're in hell."[1]

Cute story, but very misleading. The popular consensus is that all people, regardless of their spiritual convictions, will end up in the same location after they die. Any differences in after-death experiences will be only a matter of perception. But the Bible teaches just the opposite. There are two *very different* destinies awaiting individuals after they die. Jesus affirmed this truth when He said,

> "Enter by the narrow gate; for the gate is wide, and the way is broad that leads to destruction, and many are those who enter by it. For the gate is small, and the way is narrow that leads to life, and few are those who find it." (Matt. 7:13–14)

Two gates, two roads, two destinies. Up to this point, we have tracked the future of both believers and unbelievers in God's prophetic plan. We have seen that when a Christian dies his spirit will go immediately to be with Christ and his body will be resurrected at a specific time according to God's order: some at the Rapture, others at the Second Coming, and the remainder at the end of the Millennium. Not only will these Christians be resurrected, but they will also be rewarded—again at different times. Believers living in this present age (often referred to as the Church Age) will be evaluated at the judgment seat of Christ, which apparently will take place immediately after the Rapture.

Other believers will be rewarded at times not specified in Scripture. But all believers will share the same future: resurrected bodies, eternal rewards, and a re-created heaven and earth.

Sadly, unbelievers will not share in that future. Although some unbelievers (those who survive the Tribulation) will be judged at the Second Coming of Christ and cast into the eternal lake of fire, the majority of unbelievers will be raised from the dead prior to the Great White Throne Judgment. Because of their unwillingness to trust in Christ as their Savior, they will be judged by their works and cast into the eternal lake of fire where they "will be tormented day and night forever and ever" (Rev. 20:10).

In this chapter we are going to examine more closely what is often referred to as "the eternal state." What is hell going to be like for unbelievers? What can believers anticipate in heaven?

The Truth about Hell

I find it fascinating that many people who readily accept the idea of heaven just as easily dismiss the biblical teaching about hell. Robert Ingersoll, the famous lawyer and atheist in the nineteenth century, once delivered a scorching (pardon the pun) lecture on the absurdity of hell. He labeled hell as "the scarecrow of religion" and told his audience how unscientific the whole concept was. Most intelligent people, Ingersoll claimed, had long ago abandoned belief in hell. A drunk approached Ingersoll after the talk and said, "Bob, I liked your lecture about hell. But I want you to be sure about it, because I'm depending on you."[2]

Unfortunately many people are banking their eternal destiny on the wrong people. Instead of listening to the "logic" of people like Ingersoll, we should consider the words of the only Person who is capable of describing what really awaits us beyond the grave.

Jesus Christ had a great deal to say about the reality of hell. In fact, He spoke more often about hell than He did about heaven. The Lord's most extensive discourse about hell is found in Luke 16:

> "Now there was a certain rich man, and he habitually dressed in purple and fine linen, gaily living in splendor every day. And a certain poor man named Lazarus was laid at this gate, covered with sores, and longing to be fed with the crumbs which were falling from the rich man's table; besides, even the dogs were coming and licking his sores. Now it came about that the poor man died and he was carried away by the angels to Abraham's bosom; and the rich man also died and was buried. And in Hades he lifted up his eyes, being in torment, and saw Abraham far away, and Lazarus in his bosom. And he cried out and said, 'Father Abraham, have mercy on me, and send Lazarus, that he may dip the tip of his finger in water and cool off my tongue; for I am in agony in this flame.' But Abraham said, 'Child, remember that during your life you received your good

things, and likewise Lazarus bad things; but now
he is being comforted here, and you are in agony.
And besides all this, between us and you there is
a great chasm fixed, in order that those who wish
to come over from here to you may not be able,
and that none may cross over from there to us.'"
(Luke 16:19–26)

The New Testament uses three words to describe the destination of non-Christians. While all three of these words are
translated as "hell" in many English versions of the Bible, the
three Greek words denote very different places. First, the word,
Tartaros (used only in 2 Pet. 2:4), describes the place of judgment of the wicked angels described in Jude 6. The second
word, *Gehenna,* is used twelve times in the New Testament and
primarily refers to the eternal lake of fire (Rev. 19:20; 20:10,
15), which will be the final residence of all unbelievers. The
third word for *hell* is the one found in the Luke 16 passage:
Hades. The term *Hades* is used to describe the temporary location of the unsaved dead who are awaiting the Great White
Throne Judgment (Luke 16:23). You will remember that at this
judgment the residents of Hades will be resurrected and eventually dispatched to the lake of fire (*Gehenna*).[3]

Although Jesus is specifically describing Hades in this
parable (which may have been an actual incident), we can
assume that the horrors of Hades are also characteristic of the
eternal lake of fire. Thus, from this point on we will use the general term *hell* to describe the future residence of unbelievers.
What did Jesus teach about hell?

Hell Is a Place of Physical Torment

The rich man begged Abraham for mercy because he was "in agony in this flame" (Luke 16:24). There is a growing belief in a doctrine called *annihilationism,* which theorizes that unbelievers are judged and then destroyed, instead of being tormented for all eternity. While such a belief may be comforting, it is not accurate. Jesus is warning that unbelievers will face an eternity of indescribable suffering. Most of us have experienced excruciating pain before, but eventually relief came. But in hell there will be no relief. The awful truth of hell is that when a person has spent ten billion years there, he will not have reduced by one second the amount of time he has left in that horrible place. That is why hell will be a place of unending weeping, wailing, and gnashing of teeth (Luke 13:28).

Hell Is a Place of Indescribable Loneliness

The Bible teaches that hell is place of darkness (Matt. 8:12). Have you ever heard people say, "I want to go to hell so I can party with my friends"? Forget it. There will be no socializing in hell because no one will be able to see anyone or anything. Writer John Thomas has vividly imagined the horror of hell through the eyes of an unbeliever:

> After a roar of physical pain blasts him, he spends his first moments wailing and gnashing his teeth. But after a season, he grows accustomed to the pain, not that it's become tolerable, but that his capacity for it has enlarged to comprehend it, yet

not be consumed by it. Though he hurts, he is now able to think, and he instinctively looks about him. But as he looks, he sees only blackness.

In his past life he learned that if he looked long enough, a glow of light somewhere would yield definition to his surroundings. So he blinks and strains to focus his eyes, but his efforts yield only blackness. He turns and strains his eyes in another direction. He waits. He sees nothing but unyielding black ink. It clings to him, smothering and oppressing him.

Realizing that the darkness is not going to give way, he nervously begins to feel for something solid to get his bearings. He reaches for walls or rocks or trees or chairs; he stretches his legs to feel the ground and touches nothing. . . .

He hangs there, alone with his pain. Unable to touch a solid object or see a solitary thing, he begins to weep.

His sobs choke through the darkness. They become weak, then lost in hell's roar.[4]

Hell Is a Place of No Return

Perhaps the most disturbing aspect of hell is that once there, no occupant is able to leave. In Jesus' story, the rich man begged Abraham for a second chance, but the patriarch reminded him that "between us and you there is a great chasm fixed, in order that those who wish to come over from here to you may not be able, and that none may cross over from there to us" (Luke 16:26). Hell is an eternal destination. The Bible uses the same word (*forever*) to describe the eternality both of heaven and hell (see Rev. 22:5; 20:10). Again, John Thomas captured the horror of that realization:

> As time passes, he begins to do what the rich man did—he again starts to think. His first thoughts are of hope. You see, he still thinks as he did on earth, where he kept himself alive with hope. When things got bad, he always found a way out. If he felt pain, he took medicine. If he were hungry, he ate food. If he lost love, there was more love to be found.
>
> So he casts about in his mind for a plan to apply to the hope building in his chest.
>
> *Of course,* he thinks, *Jesus, the God of love, can get me out of this.*
>
> He cries out with a surge, "Jesus! Jesus! You were right! Help me! Get me out of this!"
>
> He waits, breathing hard with desperation. The sound of his voice slips into the darkness and is lost.
>
> He tries again. "I believe, Jesus! I believe now! Save me from this!" Again the darkness smothers his words.

Our sinner is not unique. Everyone in hell believes.[5]

I think it would be appropriate to move from the academic to the practical. Are you absolutely certain that if you were to die that you would escape the horrors of hell? Can you point to a time in your life when you placed your faith in the Lord Jesus Christ to save you from your sins?

What about the spiritual condition of your friends or family members? When you think of those people who sit across the breakfast table from you every morning, can you say with certainty that they will escape hell? I often think of the words of Martin Marty, renowned professor at the University of Chicago, about the reality of hell: "If people really believed in hell, they wouldn't be watching basketball games or even the television preachers. They would be out rescuing people."[6]

The Other Side of the Story

Fortunately, God has provided a way of escape from hell, and those who choose to enter through it will experience an eternity beyond what our finite minds can fathom. I have often wondered why the Bible does not give us more specific information about heaven. Perhaps it is because of our limited ability to comprehend such information. Or possibly God understands that such information would only increase our level of discontent with our earthly life. Imagine that you call your child to dinner. On the plate in front of him are spinach, meat, and carrots—all the things he *should* eat. But sitting right beside his plate is a beautiful strawberry shortcake, covered with whipped cream. It would be difficult for any child (and many adults!) to eat spinach with a strawberry shortcake in full view. If we had a clear picture of all the splendors of heaven that awaited us, we might find it difficult to concentrate on our responsibilities in this life.[7] Nevertheless, God gives us just enough information about heaven to whet our appetites for the future.

What does the Bible reveal about heaven? Once a year our church devotes a Sunday evening service to a program we call "Stump the Pastor." Church members are given the opportunity to pose any question they choose to yours truly. It is always a fun experience and is our most attended evening service of the year (people love to see their pastor squirm). Since many of the questions I am asked have to do with heaven, I thought you might be interested in the answers to the ten most frequently asked questions about the eternal state for believers.

1. Is heaven an actual place or simply a state of mind?

The Bible goes to great lengths to demonstrate that heaven is a definite place. In John 14 Jesus twice referred to heaven as a "place" (the Greek word is *topos*, denoting a specific location).

> In My Father's house are many dwelling places; if it were not so, I would have told you; for I go to prepare a *place* for you. And if I go and prepare a *place* for you, I will come again, and receive you to Myself; that where I am, there you may be also. (John 14:2–3, Author emphasis)

In the above passage Jesus also described heaven as being filled with "dwelling places," which again indicates that heaven is a definite location. Also, consider the description of Jesus' ascension into heaven:

> And after He had said these things, He was lifted up while they were looking on, and a cloud received Him out of their sight. And as they were gazing intently into the sky while He was departing, behold, two men in white clothing stood beside them; and they also said, "Men of Galilee, why do you stand looking into the sky? This Jesus, who has been taken up from you into heaven, will come in just the same way as you have watched Him go into heaven." (Acts 1:9–11)

When Jesus ascended into "heaven," where did He go? Did He ascend from reality to a "state of mind"? Of course not. The Bible is teaching that heaven is a real location.[8]

2. Where do Christians go when they die?

The Bible clearly teaches that when a Christian dies, he is "at home with the Lord" (2 Cor. 5:8). While we often use the term *heaven* to refer to destination of believers who die, it is not entirely accurate to do so. Our final heavenly home (the one referred to by Jesus in John 14 and described by John in Rev. 21–22) is still "under construction." Just as most unbelievers will not be cast into the lake of fire until after the Great White Throne Judgment, believers will not see the new heaven and earth God is constructing until after the destruction of the present heaven and earth.

3. When people die do they go to a kind of purgatory until the end of time?

As we saw in the parable of the rich man and Lazarus, when people die they go to a place known as "Hades." Until the resurrection of Christ, Hades was divided into two compartments: the place of torment for unbelievers (the destination of the rich man) and "Abraham's bosom" (the destination of Lazarus). But since Christ's resurrection, when an unbeliever dies, he immediately experiences unbearable torment as he awaits his final judgment at the Great White Throne. After that judgment he is cast into the eternal lake of fire. When a Christian dies, he immediately experiences the joy of being in God's presence until the time that he inhabits the new heaven and the new earth.

Some Bible scholars believe that Hades is still divided into "Abraham's bosom" for Christians and the "place of torment" for unbelievers. Others believe that after the resurrection of Christ, the Lord emptied the compartment known as "Abraham's bosom" and brought its inhabitants into His presence. Thus, today the term *Hades* refers only to the temporary, but nevertheless horrific, dwelling place of unbelievers. When Christians die, they go into the presence of God, wherever that might be.

What we do know with certainty is this: when unbelievers die they immediately begin to suffer; when Christians die, they are immediately transported into God's presence.

4. What is the difference between the millennial kingdom and the new heaven and new earth described in Revelation 21–22?

The millennial kingdom will involve a renovation of the present earth. But after the Great White Throne Judgment, the present heaven and earth will be completely destroyed (2 Pet. 3:7), and God will unveil His new heaven and earth. Look at John's description of this new heaven and earth:

> And I saw a new heaven and a new earth; for the first heaven and the first earth passed away, and there is no longer any sea. And I saw the holy city, new Jerusalem, coming down out of heaven from God, made ready as a bride adorned for her husband. (Rev. 21:1–2)

The final destination for Christians will be this "new Jerusalem," which John saw descending from heaven to the new earth. When John first viewed this magnificent city, it was already complete. I like to refer to the new Jerusalem as the ultimate in prefab housing! The Bible teaches that currently this city is being constructed under the supervision of Jesus Christ ("I go to prepare a place for you"), and at God's appointed time this city will descend to the new earth.

Revelation 21–22 gives us many details about this city: its great wall, its twelve gates, the twelve foundation stones, the absence of night or the sea, and the tree of life, which shall provide healing for the nations. But one of the most interesting aspects of the city is its size. John described the city as a cube that is 1,500 miles long, wide, and high (Rev. 21:16). If these measurements are to be understood literally (and the specificity of the measurements argue for a literal interpretation), then we are talking about a very large city!

My father in the ministry, Dr. W. A. Criswell, noted that such a city would stretch from Maine to Florida and would cover all of Ireland, Great Britain, France, Spain, Germany, Austria, Italy, Turkey, and half of Russia.[9] Additionally, there is no reason to think that Christians will be confined to this earthly city, given the supernatural bodies we will possess. I believe we will be free to roam the universe! So you can quit worrying that there will not be enough room in heaven for you and everyone you want to bring with you!!

5. What kind of bodies will we have in heaven? Will we know one another in heaven?

Our heavenly bodies will be both superior and, at the same time, similar to our present bodies. In 1 Corinthians 15, Paul used an agricultural analogy to illustrate this truth. When a farmer plants a seed in the ground, the seed actually dies, Miraculously, that decomposed seed produces a harvest that is superior to, and yet also similar to, the original seed. Have you ever thought how amazing it is that a tiny seed planted in the ground can eventually become a large watermelon? The harvest is certainly superior to the seed (on a hot summer day would you rather eat a cold watermelon or a watermelon seed?), and yet the harvest is similar to the seed. You don't plant a watermelon seed and harvest an orange.

Similarly, our present bodies must die before we can reap the harvest of our new bodies. Although our new bodies will be as superior to our present ones as a watermelon is to a watermelon seed, there will nevertheless be some similarities between the two.

Jesus' resurrection body illustrates the continuity that will exist between our new bodies and our old ones. Jesus' new body was certainly superior to His old one. Read Luke 24, and you will discover that Jesus' resurrection body was not limited by time and space. He could travel through walls and doors. And yet He was not just a spirit, but possessed flesh and bones that the disciples could actually touch. Amazingly, Jesus enjoyed eating in his new body (which gives me hope that just possibly there will be Haagen-Daz ice cream in heaven!).

Jesus' new body apparently retained some of the physical characteristics of His earthly body, since His disciples recognized Him. That is why we can safely assume that we, too, will recognize one another in heaven. Our bodies will not be identical to one another, but will retain some of the unique characteristics of our previous bodies.

Many years ago I visited the Boeing aircraft company in Seattle, Washington, and saw the huge assembly line where those gigantic aircraft are manufactured. Before the assembly line ever starts producing airplanes, however, the designers must build the first plane, called a "prototype." After the prototype has been built, then the other planes are patterned after the first one. The Bible tells us that Jesus' resurrection body was a prototype of the bodies we will one day receive: bodies that are superior, and yet similar, to our present ones (see Col. 1:15; 1 John 3:2).

6. What age will we be in heaven?

Although I always anticipate this question at our annual "Stump the Pastor" session, this year I was surprised by a unique variation of it. "If a woman is pregnant at the Rapture, will she be pregnant throughout eternity?" I paused and answered, "Yes—it's called hell!" After the laughter subsided, I had to admit that I don't know the answer to that question. Will embryos on earth be embryos in heaven? Will children on earth remain children in the new world? Will the American Association for Retired Persons have a branch office inside the pearly gates?

Obviously the real question is, "What age will we be in heaven?" Some have theorized that we will be the same age as the Lord when He began His earthly ministry (age thirty). But the truth is that the Bible is silent on this topic.

7. Will there be animals in heaven?

As we saw in our study of the Millennium, the Bible describes the presence of animals on the renovated earth, including the wolf, lamb, calf, and lion (Isa. 11:6–9). However, there is no mention of animals in the eternal state. If God chooses to place animals on the new earth, they will not be our present pets in resurrected bodies. Ancient civilizations believed in the resurrection of household pets and placed replicas of those pets in the tombs of the deceased. But there is no indication in Scripture that animals possess eternal spirits that can be redeemed.

8. Will there be marriage in heaven?

Jesus clearly answered this question. A group of Sadducees (who did not even believe in the afterlife) played their own version of "Stump the Rabbi" by posing this question: "If a woman has seven different husbands in this life, whose wife will she be in heaven?" Jesus replied,

> "The sons of this age marry and are given in marriage, but those who are considered worthy to attain to that age and the resurrection from the dead, neither marry, nor are given in marriage; for neither can they die anymore, for they are like angels, and are sons of God, being sons of the resurrection." (Luke 20:34–36)

Please note that Jesus did not say we *become* angels when we die, but in heaven we will share one similarity with the angels: we will not marry. You may not think you could enjoy heaven without marriage. Others may be more upset at the prospect of not having Fido with them in heaven. But remember, heaven is going to be a place of incomparable joy for every believer.

9. What will we do in heaven?

The image of Christians floating on clouds and plucking harps throughout eternity is popular but inaccurate. The parable of the talents found in Matthew 25 indicates that we will be assigned responsibilities for ruling over cities, planets, and galaxies according to our faithfulness to God in this life. Since God originally created the first couple to be workers (see

Gen. 1–2) in His creation, we can assume that we will be busy in God's new world. Fortunately, those impediments to the enjoyment of our work in this life will be removed in the next life.

10. Are Christians in heaven aware of what is happening on the earth?

Many people cite Hebrews 12:1 as evidence that deceased believers are peering over heaven's balcony and watching our every action: "Therefore, since we have so great a cloud of witnesses surrounding us, let us also lay aside every encumbrance, and the sin which so easily entangles us." However, the context of this verse demonstrates that the "cloud of witnesses" is a reference to the heroes of the faith mentioned in Hebrews 11. The writer was saying, "In light of their example of faith, we should persevere in our faith."

Nevertheless, there are some indications that people in heaven have an understanding of what is taking place on earth. Abraham was aware of the rich man's suffering in Hades (Luke 16), and the Tribulation saints will be aware of God's restraint of judgment against the earth (Rev. 6:10). The apostle Paul indicated that our perspective in this life is limited, but one day we "shall know fully" (1 Cor. 13:12). I would assume that such perfect knowledge would include a full awareness of all that is happening on earth.

A related question is, Will Christians experience grief in heaven? If Christians in heaven possess a full knowledge of events on earth, as well as the eternal damnation of some of our loved ones at the Great White Throne Judgment, doesn't that mean that there will be tears in heaven?

Revelation 21:4 promises that "[God] shall wipe away every tear from their eyes; and there shall no longer be any death; there shall no longer be any mourning, or crying, or pain; the first things have passed away." Remember that the setting for this verse is *after* the judgment seat of Christ, the Great White Throne Judgment, and the destruction of the present heaven and earth. God promises that whatever sorrow may have accrued through those events will ultimately be resolved.

A Final Thought

Just think, no more failed relationships, no more all-night vigils at the hospital, no more standing over the open grave of a loved one, no more crying or pain! I don't know about you, but that thought makes me want to push aside the spinach and grab some of that strawberry shortcake! Obviously, God is not ready for us to do that just yet. He has given us some responsibilities in this world that must be fulfilled before we can enjoy the next one. In fact, the unpleasantness of this life will serve to make heaven taste that much better. But the opposite is true as well. The assurance of a better world should improve the taste of this one.

One of the most frequent criticisms of studying Bible prophecy is that it has no relevance to this life. Haven't you heard the cliché, "It is possible to be so heavenly-minded that you are of no earthly good"? Yet the Bible never divorces the hope of the next life from our responsibility in this one. Peter wrote,

> Since all these things are to be destroyed in this way, what sort of people ought you to be in holy

conduct and godliness, looking for and hastening
the coming of the day of God! (2 Pet. 3:11–12)

Shouldn't the truth of the Rapture affect our attitude
toward our money, which we will one day be forced to leave
behind? Shouldn't the reality of the Great White Throne
Judgment motivate us to share Christ with those around us?
Shouldn't the certainty of the Judgment Seat of Christ impact
how we invest our time and energy?

I close with these words of C. S. Lewis about the value of
being "heavenly-minded":

> Hope is one of the theological virtues. This means
> that a continual looking forward to the eternal
> world is not as some moderns think a form of
> escapism or wishful thinking but one of the things
> a Christian is meant to do. It does not mean that
> we are to leave the present world as it is. If you
> read history you will find that the Christians who
> did most for the present world were just those who
> thought most of the next. It is since Christians
> have largely ceased to think of the other world that
> they have become so ineffective in this one.
>
> Aim at heaven and you will get earth thrown in.
> Aim at earth and you will get neither.

Good words to remember . . . as time runs out.

Study Questions

Chapter 1: Why Study Prophecy?

1. What are the most common reasons people avoid studying prophecy? Which of these excuses have you used?

2. How would you answer someone who said, "Studying prophecy is a waste of time since the Bible says no one can know when Christ will return"?

3. Does the fact that there are a variety of opinions about end-time events make the study of prophecy futile? Why or why not?

4. Briefly summarize the three reasons, found in this chapter, for studying prophecy.

5. Give one example in which an understanding of end-time events could impact your everyday life.

6. Give one example in which a clear understanding of prophecy would assist you in interpreting a passage of Scripture accurately.

7. Why did you purchase this book? What do you hope this study of prophecy will do for you?

Chapter 2: Promises, Promises

1. According to the author, what is the major theme of the Bible (Gen. 12–Rev. 22)?

2. What does the story of Abraham teach us about God's grace?

3. What are the three ingredients of God's promise to Abraham? Briefly describe each one.

4. Explain what Abraham understood about a coming Savior. Support your answer with Scripture.

5. Explain the term *reckon* as it relates to Christ's death. How would you illustrate this concept to a nine-year-old?

6. List and briefly explain the three characteristics of God's covenant with Abraham.

7. Why should we care whether or not God keeps His promises to Israel?

8. Of all of God's promises, which one is the most important to you? Why?

Chapter 3: Getting the Big Picture

1. Arrange these end-time events in the correct order (according to the viewpoint presented in this chapter). Place *1* by the first event, 2 by the second event, and so on.

Second Coming of Christ
Tribulation
The Church Age
Eternity
The Millennium
The Rapture
The Great White Throne Judgment

2. Have you ever studied Bible prophecy before? Why or why not?

3. Now that you have read this chapter, see if you can give a one-or two-sentence explanation for each of these terms:

Church Age:

Rapture:

Tribulation:

Second Coming:

Millennium:

Great White Throne Judgment:

Eternity:

4. How did Jesus answer His disciples' questions about the end times? What can we learn from His reply?

Chapter 4: Not Left Behind

1. Explain the "mystery" that the apostle Paul unveiled.

2. Why didn't the Old Testament writers of Jesus mention the Rapture?

3. How has Israel's rejection of Christ benefited those of us who are Gentiles?

4. Cite one significant difference between the Rapture and the Second Coming of Christ.

5. In your own words summarize what will take place at the Rapture.

6. Does cremation or organ donation jeopardize our new bodies in heaven? Why or why not?

7. Briefly explain the differing views of the Rapture. Which view do you believe? Why?

8. Four arguments are given for a pretribulation Rapture of the Church. Which of these arguments seems most convincing to you?

Chapter 5: When All Hell Breaks Loose

1. What important information does Daniel 9 reveal about the Tribulation?

2. What occurs between the first 483 years and the final 7 years of God's plan for Israel?

3. Define "the day of the Lord."

4. What do we learn about "the day of the Lord" from 1 Thessalonians 5:1–4?

5. The author described the Tribulation as occurring in three "acts." Summarize the action of each of these acts:

Act One: The Beginning

Act Two: The Middle

Act Three: The Final Half of the Tribulation

6. What are God's two purposes for the Tribulation?

7. How is God's mercy demonstrated through the 144,000 Jewish witnesses?

8. In one or two sentences, summarize the activity of the Antichrist during the Tribulation.

Chapter 6: Here Comes the Bride

1. Briefly summarize the events we have studied so far in this book, including:

The Abrahamic Covenant:

The Church Age:

The Rapture:

The Tribulation:

2. What will be the human explanation for the battle called Armageddon? What will be the divine purpose for this conflict?

3. Describe what Christians will do at Armageddon.

4. Why do some people view the Rapture and Second Coming of Christ as the same event?

5. Cite three or four differences between the Rapture and the Second Coming.

6. Why is a literal return of Jesus Christ to earth important?

7. What excites you most about the Second Coming of Christ? Why?

Chapter 7: Heaven on Earth

1. Define the word *Millennium*:

2. What reasons does the author give for believing in a literal thousand-year reign of Christ?

3. Briefly summarize these basic positions:
• premillennialism:

• postmillennialism:

• amillennialism:

4. Which viewpoint best expresses your belief? Why?

5. What do you see as the major problem with your particular millennial viewpoint?

6. How does a person's belief about the Millennium impact his understanding of other portions of the Bible?

7. What is the difference between the premillennial and amillennial understanding of the Abrahamic Covenant?

8. Compare and contrast the Millennium with the new heaven and new earth.

Chapter 8:
The Great White Throne Judgment

1. Explain the difference between the first resurrection and the second resurrection.

2. How is the first resurrection like a military parade (or car pool)?

3. When does the author believe that we who are living in the Church Age will receive our new bodies? How will our bodies differ from those of the Tribulation survivors during the Millennium?

4. Why will God release Satan at the end of the Millennium? Identify those whom Satan will deceive.

5. If someone were to ask you, "How do you know Christians cannot lose their salvation?" how would you respond?

6. Summarize the following about the Great White Throne Judgment:

The participants in this judgment:

The basis for this judgment:

The result of this judgment:

7. Why will unbelievers be judged by their works at the Great White Throne Judgment?

Chapter 9: Rewards in Heaven

1. Identify the participants at the Judgment Seat of Christ.

2. What makes this judgment different from the Great White Throne Judgment?

3. How would you answer someone who asked, "How could God judge me for my mistakes, since they have been forgiven by Christ?"

4. By what standards will Christians be evaluated at the Judgment Seat of Christ?

5. Can our good works earn God's approval? Explain.

6. What rewards can be earned at the judgment seat of Christ?

7. Describe the loss some Christians will suffer at the Judgment Seat of Christ.

8. As you reflect on this chapter, what specific changes could you make in your life right now to ensure future rewards?

Chapter 10: The Truth about Eternity

1. What is the most common misconception people have about life after death?

2. What does Jesus' story about the rich man and Lazarus (Luke 16) reveal to us about hell?

3. How would you answer someone who said, "I don't believe a loving God would punish unbelievers forever"?

4. Why doesn't the Bible teach us more about heaven?

5. How do we know that heaven is an actual location rather than a state of mind?

6. Imagine you are speaking to a ten-year-old. Trace what happens to a Christian's spirit and body from the time he dies until the time of the new heaven and earth.

7. Why does the author believe we will recognize one another in heaven?

8. What aspect of heaven most appeals to you? Why?

Notes

Chapter 1

1. Paul Aurandt, *Paul Harvey's The Rest of the Story* (New York: Bantam Books, 1977), 43–45.

2. Billy Graham, speech at the Southern Baptist Convention, St. Louis, June 1987.

Chapter 2

1. Quoted by Russ Crosson in *A Life Well Spent* (Nashville: Thomas Nelson, 1994), 3.

Chapter 4

1. Charles C. Ryrie, *What You Should Know about the Rapture* (Chicago: Moody Press, 1981), 44.

2. Ibid., 28.

Chapter 5

1. Billy Graham, *Till Armageddon* (Waco, Tex.: Word Books, 1981), 7.

2. Aliza Marcus, "Jews, Muslims at Odds over Holy Shrine," *Wichita Falls Times Record News,* 27 October 1998, 3a.

3. J. Dwight Pentecost, *Things to Come* (Grand Rapids, Mich.: Zondervan, 1964), 246.

4. Adam Rogers, "Attention: Incoming Objects," *Newsweek,* 24 March 1997, 64.

5. My summary of the trumpet, seal, and bowl judgments is based, in part, on material from my former professor, Dr. John Walvoord, and is explained in detail in his book, *The Revelation of Jesus Christ* (Chicago: Moody Press, 1966).

Chapter 6

1. William Martin, *A Prophet with Honor* (New York: William Morrow and Company, 1991), 281.

2. Ryrie, *What You Should Know,* 43–46.

3. Michael P. Green, *Illustrations for Biblical Preaching* (Grand Rapids, Mich.: Baker Book House, 1982), 434–35.

Chapter 7

1. "Dear Abby," *The Dallas Morning News,* 15 January 1991, 6c.

2. Charles Ryrie, *The Basis for the Premillennial Faith* (Neptune, N.J.: Loizeaux Brothers Inc., 1953), 12.

Chapter 8

1. Author's file, source unknown.

2. Pentecost, *Things to Come,* 402.

3. Erwin W. Lutzer, *How You Can Be Sure That You Will Spend Eternity with God* (Chicago: Moody Press, 1996), 67–68.

Chapter 9

1. Joe L. Wall, *Going for the Gold* (Chicago: Moody Press, 1991), 9–10.

2. Ibid., 87.

3. George F. Will, "The Gospel from Science," *Newsweek,* 9 November 1998, 88.

4. Robert Jeffress, *Say Goodbye to Regret* (Sisters, Oreg.: Multnomah, 1998), 19–20.

5. Erwin W. Lutzer, *Your Eternal Reward* (Chicago: Moody Press, 1998), 80.

Chapter 10

1. Harold Kushner, *When All You've Ever Wanted Isn't Enough* (New York: Simon and Schuster, 1986), 156–57.

2. Quoted by Billy Graham in *Facing Death* (Waco, Tex.: Word, 1987), 36.

3. Pentecost, *Things to Come,* 555–60.

4. John Thomas, "That Hideous Doctrine," *Moody Monthly,* September 1985, 92.

5. Ibid.

6. *U.S. News and World Report,* 25 March 1991, 56.

7. Charles Allen, *When You Lose a Loved One* (Westwood, N.J.: Fleming H. Revell, 1959), 57–58.

8. W. A. Criswell and Paige Patterson, *Heaven* (Wheaton, Ill.: Tyndale House, 1991), 5–6.

9. W. A. Criswell, *Expository Sermons on Revelation* (Grand Rapids, Mich.: Zondervan, 1969), 129.